Cambridge Elements

Elements in Eighteenth-Century Connections
edited by
Eve Tavor Bannet
University of Oklahoma
Markman Ellis
Queen Mary University of London

ON WONDER

Literature and Science in the Long Eighteenth Century

Tita Chico
University of Maryland

CAMBRIDGE
UNIVERSITY PRESS

Shaftesbury Road, Cambridge CB2 8EA, United Kingdom

One Liberty Plaza, 20th Floor, New York, NY 10006, USA

477 Williamstown Road, Port Melbourne, VIC 3207, Australia

314–321, 3rd Floor, Plot 3, Splendor Forum, Jasola District Centre, New Delhi – 110025, India

103 Penang Road, #05–06/07, Visioncrest Commercial, Singapore 238467

Cambridge University Press is part of Cambridge University Press & Assessment, a department of the University of Cambridge.

We share the University's mission to contribute to society through the pursuit of education, learning and research at the highest international levels of excellence.

www.cambridge.org
Information on this title: www.cambridge.org/9781009539678

DOI: 10.1017/9781108874618

When citing this work, please include a reference to the DOI 10.1017/9781108874618

First published 2025

A catalogue record for this publication is available from the British Library

ISBN 978-1-009-53967-8 Hardback
ISBN 978-1-108-79264-6 Paperback
ISSN 2632-5578 (online)
ISSN 2632-556X (print)

On Wonder

Literature and Science in the Long Eighteenth Century

Elements in Eighteenth-Century Connections

DOI: 10.1017/9781108874618
First published online: January 2025

Tita Chico
University of Maryland

Author for correspondence: Tita Chico, tchico@umd.edu

Abstract: This is an Element about wonder – as an object, as a feeling, as an invitation to study, and as a way of thinking in both literary and scientific texts of the long eighteenth century. Wonder is at the heart of natural philosophical inquiry in the long eighteenth century, its inaugural provocation, its long-standing problematic. Yet wonder requires observation and imagination, operating together, if uneasily, to give shape to forms of scientific, literary, and social knowledge, shaping how thinking works – and who can do it. Studying wonder in the long eighteenth century helps us to understand our current disciplinary configurations, and also how wonder itself embodies the potential for a more capacious critical practice. Studying wonder as an epistemology, praxis, and thematic in the long eighteenth century also carries the promise of invigorating and reimagining our own critical, creative endeavors.

Keywords: wonder, literature, science, awe, natural world

ISBNs: 9781009539678 (HB), 9781108792646 (PB), 9781108874618 (OC)
ISSNs: 2632-5578 (online), 2632-556X (print)

Contents

1 Why Wonder

On Monday, 5 July 2021, my 89-year-old mother had a hemorrhagic stroke, commonly known as a "brain bleed." Her move to Washington DC delayed by COVID, she had just spent her first night alone when the blood vessels in her mind burst. I will always be baffled and grateful that she somehow was able to dial me on her new telephone to tell me that she couldn't see the salmon on her plate at lunch and that the numbers on the elevator had been floating around.

The doctors, once they scanned her brain, could see where the hemorrhagic stroke occurred – it was the size of a quarter, straddling the right parietal and occipital lobes. And based on that location, they knew the left quadrant of her field of vision was damaged. The neurologist showed us the MRI of my mother's brain, pointing to the dark streaks and smudges marking where this and her previous strokes occurred. That MRI offered an image of what happened to my mother's brain. That MRI offered, from the neurologist's point of view, an explanation for her loss of vision.

But that explanation offered little comfort to my mother. Even after several days in the Intensive Care Unit, with significant vision loss, frail, and at times disoriented, my mother was still sharp witted, trained in the 1960s in the History of Ideas Program at Johns Hopkins in Baltimore.

My mother looked from the MRI to the neurologist and said, "But that doesn't explain what a thought is."

The medical explanation of her brain, in other words, did not displace the wonder – the awe and the questioning – at the heart of her response. That grainy, black-and-white photograph does not explain what had happened to her any more than it explains what it means to be human. Steeped as we are in a culture that turns to science to explain our world to ourselves, the hold of wonder, in some ways inexplicably, persists. Even *The New York Times* has taken note (Reese, 2023).

My mother's response captures the wonder of her own experience of a stroke. It also signals the curiosity – the intellectual desire to know more – at the heart of any experience of wonder. In a 1734 poem, *ΓΝΩΘΙ ΣΕΑΥΤΟΝ, Know Your Self*, John Arbuthnot likewise grapples with the explanatory power of science. The poet asks if he is merely an object filled with veins and arteries pumping blood, as microscopy teaches: "Am I but what I seem, mere Flesh and Blood; / A branching Channel, with a mazy Flood?" (Arbuthnot, 1734: 2). This cannot be, Arbuthnot's poet insists, for "the purple Stream that through my Vessels glides" and "The Pipes thro' which the circling Juices stray, / Are not that thinking I, no more than They" (Arbuthnot, 1734: 2).

"This Frame," he concludes, "I call it Mine, not Me" (Arbuthnot, 1734: 2). My mother's MRI-scanned brain, she concludes, is hers, not her.

Why wonder.

The long eighteenth-century textual landscape is populated by wonders and by wondering: one encounters seemingly countless objects of wonder and just as many experiences of wonder.[1] These texts take up wonder as a noun and a verb, as an object and feeling, as an experience both emotional and intellectual. They also imagine wonder in relation to emergent notions of scientific practice and accounts of the natural world writ large. There are reports of groaning trees; individuals who lived to upwards of 140 years; a "Tartar Lamb," or a "Vegetable Lamb," part animal, part vegetable; the moon bleeding; a tiny bird with a warble that shakes a gazebo; an insect that lives three years but also lives one day; a white Dutch boy with legible Latin and Hebrew inscribed in his eyes; a white Devonshire woman whose legs self-amputate; an enslaved Black African man in the Middle Passage seeing an expansive world through a quadrant immediately before reaching the horrific human marketplace of Barbados.

While the specifics may differ in tenor and tone, inquiry and conclusion, these texts reveal the power and interest that *wonder* as a concept conveyed in the British long eighteenth century. These are all objects that provoke wonder in those who witness or learn about them, they generate a desire for narrative and explanation, and they invite us to see differently and to imagine a world otherwise. I borrow the phrase "imagine otherwise" from Kandice Chuh, who demonstrates the importance of continuing to use terms in ways that foreground their usefulness and limitations, their historicity and futures: to think otherwise is to ground a theory of knowledge in the messiness of incommensurability (Chuh, 2003: x). For Eugenia Zuroski, these are the "funny things" that call out to us from the eighteenth-century archive, that point to absurd, chimerical details – the groaning tree in Hampshire is certainly one. These things are not only "glitches in cultural logic" but also portals to other, more just ways of knowing and being (Zuroski, 2025 in press). The texts I discuss throughout remind us that wonder is a noun and a verb. They also reveal to us that wonder is a set of relations and arguments for knowledge making, a way of studying the natural world and seeing one's place in it. As a set of possibilities and relations, wonder teaches us that the affective, epistemological, and social are inevitably intertwined, resulting in entanglements that demand our critical attention.

[1] Jean Céard's classic study, *La nature et les prodigies: l'insolite au 16e siècle, en France* (Geneva: Droz, 1977), focuses on wonders as features of popular culture.

Why wonder.

"However certain the facts or any science may be, and however just the ideas we may have formed of these facts, we can only communicate false or imperfect impressions of these ideas to others, while we want words by which they may be properly expressed" (Lavoisier, 1790: xv).

Why wonder.

Wonder makes visible things and relations, values and ideals, limitations and possibilities. Wonder is simultaneously observational and imaginative, in ways that natural philosophy reproduces but also obscures. What makes my book different is that wonder not only provokes scientific inquiry but also makes *science* visible as a theory, as a practice, as an embodied domain of knowledge. Others have argued that attending to the politics of natural philosophical inquiry reveals the processes whereby how one knows becomes inextricable from who one is (Shapin and Schaffer, 1985: 15, 283; Latour, 1993: 27; Harding, 2008: 36–48). But I take this further. Drawing upon Ian Hacking's thought, I view science as a way of organizing knowledge, peoples, and institutions; it is to reimagine science as a "doing" that both institutes and forecloses relations (Hacking, 1983: 173; Chico, 2024: 472). Considering science as a set of relations helps us to understand its entanglement with wonder. Robert T. Pennock observes that "Science, like all great philosophy, begins in wonder"; moreover, "the secret to science is wondering in a special way" (Pennock, 2019: 1). From the long eighteenth century to today, the nexus of wonder and science demands our attention.

Katherine McKittrick's *Dear Science and Other Stories* inspires wonder – and wonder and science – in these pages, as does Kandice Chuh's *The Difference Aesthetics Makes*. The "science" of *Dear Science* is extricable from wonder. In the main, McKittrick attends to the construction of knowledge and, pressingly, the "humanizing work [of] black creatives . . . in their scientifically creative and creatively scientific artworlds" (McKittrick, 2021: 2). McKittrick explains the "science" of the book's title as "a shadow, a story, a friendship. Science reveals failed attachments" (McKittrick, 2021: 3, n. 5). The relations of science – the relations that define science – include the alignments that buttress its truth claims as a liberal, Enlightenment epistemology just as much as those that reveal what Kandice Chuh calls "illiberal humanisms." Illiberal humanisms are, Chuh explains, "directed toward the protection and flourishing of people and of ways of being and knowing and of inhabiting the planet that liberal humanism, wrought through the defining structures of modernity, tries so hard to extinguish" (Chuh, 2019: 2). These people, these ways of being and knowing and inhabiting – together they show us *relations*: therefore, in Chuh's formulation, "Relationality, as this book suggests, is as much a principle for organizing knowledge production as it is a reference to a condition of being" (Chuh, 2019: 5). Natural philosophy – science writ large – can be understood as an instrument of the Enlightenment, as instrumental. If, broadly speaking, science seems to accrue the status of truth (although many were skeptical from the moment of its emergence up to the modern day), then the explicit and implicit ontological claims of science can blind us to its manufacture.

Reading science through, as, and provoked by wonder opens up the possibility for us to apprehend the illiberal humanisms that are equally part of science's legacy as well as its potential, wherein, as Chuh instructs, "mastery is displaced by the prompt to collective thought and subjects (critics) and objects (texts) are understood in their mutuality" (Chuh, 2019: 5). "Unthinking mastery," as Julietta Singh argues, requires a dismantling of the drive for intellectual and, by extension, social mastery associated with the subjection inherent to colonial epistemologies and systems (Singh, 2018: 3). Wonder, as Sara Ahmed teaches us, opens up "a different relation to the world in which we live" (Ahmed, 2004: 178).

If, in McKittrick's words, "Science reveals failed attachments," then wonder offers the possibility of reimagining them. For McKittrick, anticolonial thought and Black studies provide "a way of living, and an analytical frame, that is curious and *sustained by wonder (the desire to know)*" (McKittrick, 2021: 5; emphasis added). Wonder offers a mode not only for intellectual inquiry but also for inhabiting ourselves and our worlds: "Wonder is study" (McKittrick, 2021: 5).[2]

"Wonder is study" results in the book *Dear Science and Other Stories*. The science of the book's title, in the end, is the inescapable of our shared condition, suggesting its preciousness ("dear") and the logics of intimacy and relationality ("dear"). Concluding in the epistolary mode with a letter addressed "Dear Science," McKittrick explains "that we are not outside science, we are of

[2] As McKittrick anticipates in *Dear Science*, her work could be imagined as *undisciplined* in the ways Christina Sharpe advocates: "The work we do requires new modes and methods of research and teaching" (Sharpe, 2016: 13). Zuroski, for example, takes up Sharpe's call to argue that the undisciplined eighteenth century is a necessary corrective to the field's long-standing investments in whiteness and colonial extraction (Zuroski, 2025 in press). For another enactment, see Alison Twells, Will Pooley, Matt Houlbrook, and Helen Rogers' "Undisciplined History: Creative Methods and Academic Practice" (2023). In contrast, McKittrick cautions that "undisciplined" is potentially undermining; she offers instead that "Our undoing is practiced, patient, focused" (McKittrick, 2021: 5, n. 12). Therefore, although McKittrick, Sharpe, and Zuroski share a similar goal, the way there is paved either through wonder or through the undisciplined.

science, and that the book holds in it mnemonics that repeat and restore not dehumanization but unfurled and hidden ideas about collaboration and liberation. This is where you, Science, took me" (McKittrick, 2021: 186).

This is where you, Science, took me.

My purpose is to bring wonder as an object and an affect, as a sensation that leaves one awestruck and also as an active desire to acquire knowledge, into our collective view. I take up wonder to think about its proliferation, significance, and endurance as an object of one's contemplation and one's reaction to that same object. I study wonder to understand its roles as an affective and intellectual experience, as integral to developing notions of scientific knowledge and imaginative writing. It contains the potential for us to imagine more equitable social relations and ethical reading practices. Studying wonder in the long eighteenth century helps us to understand our current disciplinary configurations. Studying wonder as an epistemology, praxis, and thematic carries the promise of invigorating and reimagining our own critical, creative endeavors, our own critical, creative relations.

McKittrick closes *Dear Science and Other Stories*: "I asked for help. People shared and collaborated generously. We are curious. I want to sustain wonder" (McKittrick, 2021: 187).

Like McKittrick before me, "I asked for help. People shared and collaborated generously. We are curious. I want to sustain wonder" (McKittrick, 2021: 187).

2 Defining Wonder

I am going to tell you a story of wonder, the "Hampshire wonder."

In 1742, a large, soaring oak in Hampshire's New Forest, close to the village of Lymington on the west bank of the Lymington River, begins to make unusual and startling noises. To the human ear, these sounds are not the usual creaks and crackles of a tree. They seem like massive sighs, "amazing groans" even (P.Q., 1742: 2). This is not a one-off occurrence, reported by a single, unverified witness, but instead an ongoing phenomenon that has been collectively observed "by Thousands of People." Local residents are alarmed. Visitors travel "from all Parts to hear this amazing and portentous Noise" (P.Q., 1742: title page). These include the author of a pamphlet entitled *The Hampshire Wonder; or, the Groaning Tree*, who is identified on the title page as "P.Q.," a Fellow of the Royal Society. P.Q. tells us that some listeners hear an intelligible lament, believing the tree to cry, "'O Walp! – Walp! It is thou that makest not only me but the whole nation to groan'" (P.Q., 1742: 5). And P.Q. reports that others describe the tree's sound as similar to "a human creature in the agonies of death, for several hours together" (P.Q., 1742: 4). The effect of the "groaning tree" on those who hear its noise is equally dramatic. "So terrifying to the Ear of human Mortals, that it astonishes the very Clergy themselves who have been to listen"; many require "proper Cordials ... to revive their sinking Spirits and confounded Imaginations" (P.Q., 1742: 2, 4).

The story of the 1742 Hampshire tree is a story of wonder.

But what is "wonder"?

As a noun, wonder is an object or a phenomenon as much as it is a feeling. And as a verb, wonder is the experience of that feeling as much as it is to think.

As a noun, a wonder is "a strange thing; something more or greater than can be expected" (Johnson, 1755: s.v. 2). It is "something that causes astonishment" (*OED*, 1989: s.v. 1). As an object, the Hampshire tree is a wonder because it emits inexplicable noises that shock and surprise listeners. And the feeling of wonder is a reaction to an object of wonder. For Samuel Johnson, this wonder is "admiration," the anglicized version of the French "l'admiration" that Descartes uses to name wonder a century earlier. Johnson views wonder as "astonishment; amazement; surprise caused by something unusual or unexpected" (Johnson, 1755: s.v. 2). As a feeling, wonder is the "emotion excited by the perception of something novel and unexpected, or inexplicable" (*OED*, 1989: s.v. II.7.a). Wonder as an affective response occurs when "astonishment mingles with perplexity or bewildered curiosity" (*OED*, 1989: s.v. II.7.a).

As these definitions imply, the noun "wonder" conveys a relationship between an object and a subject: one produces the other. The question is this: If the villagers of Lymington and all those visitors were not astonished by its sounds, would the Hampshire tree be a wonder? No, it would not. For an object to acquire the status of a wonder, it needs to produce the feeling of wonder in those who witness it.

The case of the Hampshire tree exemplifies this relation: the tree is a wonder because the people who hear its peculiar sounds are stunned and astonished, surprised beyond measure – they experience wonder.

Why does this matter? An object is considered a wonder only if it induces the feeling of wonder (admiration; astonishment; surprise) in another sentient entity. To describe an object as a wonder binds the object or phenomenon to the effect it produces, just as describing the feeling of wonder does to the object or phenomenon. Moreover, when an object or phenomenon induces this feeling, the term "wonder" is assigned *retrospectively* to the object or phenomenon; a wonder as an object is belated. Wonder not only conveys a duration; it is also a process, a relationship between objects and subjects. The frontispiece of *The Hampshire Wonder* visualizes these links, gathering everything into one frame:

clusters of men and women gather in front of the church and chickens and roosters roam in the foreground, while in the background, the titular object of wonder – an oversized, almost menacing tree – looms.

When wonder converts into a verb, we see these entanglements in action, the process and its duration in view.

In the first, "to wonder" connotes experiencing a feeling in response to an unexpected object or phenomenon; it is "to be struck with admiration; to be pleased or surprised so as to be astonished" (Johnson, 1755: s.v.). This astonishment, for many in the eighteenth century, is understood as being physically embodied. John Drummond, for example, enjoins actors to appear wide-eyed, either staring upwards at the sky or "oftener, and more expressively, fixe[d] . . . on the object . . . with the look (all except wildness) of fear" (Drummond, 1780: 26). Aaron Hill, too, encourages a similar approach: "the nerves upon a start of apprehension brace, at once, into an involuntary rigour of intenseness – under a defensive disposition of the Will – that wou'd resist, and repel, the object," "arresting the breath, eyes, gesture, and every power and faculty of the body," and "leaving an alarm upon the muscles" (Hill, 1779: 286). Tobias Smollett (1989) employs this meaning of wonder satirically in *The History and Adventures of an Atom* (first published in 1769), when the narrator, one Nathaniel Peacock, undergoes these affective responses upon hearing a voice coming from his own head, which turns out to be the atom of the volume's title: "My knees knocked together: my teeth chattered: mine hair bristled up so as to raise a cotton night-cap from the scalp: my tongue cleaved to the roof of my mouth: my temples were bedewed with a cold sweat" (Smollett, 1989: 5). (And in true Smollett fashion, the atom responds with a fart joke: "ten millions of atoms were dispersed in air by that odoriferous gale, which the commotion of thy fear produced" [Smollett, 1989: 6].)

To wonder is to experience heightened physiological responses that reflect astonishment. To wonder is a reaction – to be *struck* by something, leaving one's body and mind subjected to the effect of an external stimulus.

However, *to wonder* is not solely to feel startled or astonished. It is, in this second definition, also to think, "to ask oneself in wonderment; to feel some doubt or curiosity (how, whether, why, etc.); to be desirous to know or learn" (*OED*, 1989: s.v. 2). When Hill calls wonder "inquisitive fear," his choice of adjective signals the term's intellectual terrain (Hill, 1779: 286). The meaning of *to wonder* as an intellectual act, as "perplexed astonishment," emerged in English in the thirteenth century (Onions, 1966: s.v., "wonder"). And if wonder as thinking critically, in English, is an old term, then as an intellectual concept, it is even older. The foundational association between wonder and knowledge production layers the Western intellectual tradition beginning with Plato, who argues in *Theatetus* that "the sense of wonder is the mark of the philosopher" (Plato, 1901: 155d 2 ff), and Aristotle, who contends in *Metaphysics* that "It is owing to their wonder that men both now begin and at first began to philosophize," particularly about the natural world (Aristotle, 1984: 1.2, 982b12–22).

While some might skirt this connotation of the term's meaning (DeMaria, Jr., 2018: 5–7; Cuillé, 2021: 29–31), Sarah Tindal Kareem argues that wonder "encompasses both stupefaction – 'Ah!' – and recognition – 'Aha!'" (Kareem, 2014: 8). This matters because the concept of wonder allows one to enjoy strange and new things *and* to think about them critically, "maintaining … one's ability to question and learn" (Kareem, 2014: 9). For Kareem, this interplay between wondering *at* and wondering *about* has profound consequences for understanding the emergence and development of eighteenth-century fiction, particularly the novel. The possibilities of wonder, and the ways that its epistemology transforms over the eighteenth century, are similar to the possibilities afforded by fiction as *it* transforms over the same time period (Kareem, 2014: 10). As fictionality comes to be accepted, contends Kareem, novelists turn from presenting their works as strange but true early in the eighteenth century (i.e., wonders as marvels) to producing wonder by means of their aesthetic virtuosity later (i.e., intricate and suspenseful plotting) (Kareem, 2014: 14).

The doubled sense of wonder as a verb – as both an affective and an epistemological response – appears in a 1739 treatise, *The Doctrine of Passion*, published by Isaac Watts, now most famous for creating English hymnology. To describe wonder, Watt first postulates that the action of wonder is physically embodied. To be astonished, that is, manifests in the subject's body:

> this passion discovers itself by lifting up of the Hands or the Eyes, and by an intense Fixation of the Sight or the Thoughts. When it rises very high on a sudden, it will stop the Voice, and reduce the Person as it were to the fixed Posture and Silence of a Statue for a few Moments, this is called *Stupor*. (Watts, 1739: 18)

Watts' verb assigns agency to "this passion" rather than to the individual experiencing it, particularly notable as the individual apparently undergoes a physical transformation. By becoming transfixed, and thus seemingly immobile, Watts presents a living, breathing human that transforms into statuary – silent and still. This is wonder as astonishment, shocking the body out of itself. However, the experience of wonder is also an experience of the mind insofar as wonder "discovers itself … by an intense Fixation … of the *Thoughts*" (emphasis added). And Watts concludes with a definitional statement modifying that stillness with a term that *means* thinking. When Watts writes of the "fixed Posture and Silence of a Statue for a few Moments," he clarifies that "This is called Stupor." Stupor is not a state of dull insensibility, as we would understand it today, but instead a stimulated and highly cognitive experience and a synonym for "wonder" as thinking. In the example of Watts, wonder is an action that variously represents interrelated desires – to feel, to be curious, to think.

To return to *The Hampshire Wonder*: the story of the 1742 Hampshire tree is a story of wonder. The pamphlet describes the phenomenon, that new and strange object of a groaning tree and, in the process, narrates the concurrent meanings of the verb "to wonder" as affect and epistemology. For P.Q., the author, those he encounters in person, and those he addresses in print, wonder produces both astonishment and a desire to know what causes the tree's noises. The two verbal connotations of wonder profoundly shape the text: if the affective quality of wonder provokes the narrative, then its epistemological connotations sustain it. As a result, the pamphlet's narrative arc unfolds wonder as a process of critical thinking, presenting accounts one by one on the way to presenting the apparently true cause.

With an explanatory narrative logic, the textual agenda of *The Hampshire Wonder* differs from what we have come to understand as novels, including those early, self-identified "strange but true" fictions as well as mid-century texts committed to their structural intricacy that Kareem studies. Instead, a text such as *The Hampshire Wonder* demonstrates that the impetus to think critically is also the impetus to explain. And in the case of the noisy tree, possible answers come from two opposing epistemes: the supernatural and the natural philosophical.

Speculative, fantastical, supernatural reports circulate among the citizens of Lymington and the thousands who visit. These include claims that the tree is a zoophyte, a version of the human-looking Mandrake; "some of the Antipodes . . . coming up"; the ghost of a man who buried his treasure under the tree; and endowed with human emotions and the ability to speak (P.Q., 1742: 5). Ghosts, unsurprisingly, appear in all manner of texts about wonder.[3] And the final possibility P.Q. mentions – that the tree is somehow human – takes

[3] For example, *The Buckinghamshire Miracle; or, the World's Wonder* features a ghost who warns a friend that he has only thirteen days left to live (*Buckinghamshire*, n.d.: titlepage), and *The Amazing Wonder; or a Full and True Relation* describes a boy who goes insane after reading words apparently drafted by a ghost, "*Come to me and I will give you rest*," words that were "neither Writ nor Printed, but had a seeming Impression" on a piece of paper ("Amazing Wonder," 1710: 6).

root because some witnesses claim to hear intelligible English in its noises, evidenced in the sentence mentioned earlier, "O Walp! – Walp! It is thou that makest not only me but the whole nation to groan" (P.Q., 1742: 5). These witnesses conclude that the tree is "undoubtedly dissatisfied with its present Situation" (P.Q., 1742: 3). P.Q. does not relay more information, which keeps open the possibility that the tree's so-called dissatisfaction could be related to any number of specific conditions (there were numerous new enclosure acts controlling the New Forest that were designed to provide lumber for the Royal Navy – is the tree groaning for its brethren?) or even a general malaise. More than the other explanations, the notion that the tree is unhappy, and cries about it, gains traction. This explanation fuels the community's fear that the tree might uproot itself and tear through the village, destroying the chapel and everything in its path. Such a possibility might seem outlandish, the narrator admits, but we learn that the villagers' apprehension seems to have historical precedent. Richard Baker's 1643 *Chronicle of the Kings of England* documents a similarly groaning tree, which, from 17 to 19 February 1571, was reported to have ripped through the countryside "with the like force it thrust before it Highwayes, Sheep-folds, Hedges and Trees, made tilled ground Pasture, and again turned Pasture into Tillage," tearing down that village's chapel (Baker, 1643: 117).

Given P.Q.'s self-identification as a FRS, it is no surprise that a natural philosophical explanation triumphs. With each account that hews to the supernatural, P.Q.'s rejection is as swift as it is pointed: these cannot be true, he argues, because they are all "unphilosophical Notions" (P.Q., 1742: 6). P.Q. promises to "clear up certain Matters of Fact relating to the Time and Manner of [the tree's] groaning" first by evaluating – and rejecting – other natural philosophical possibilities (P.Q., 1742: 6). To the claim that the noises are caused by the tree's branches moving in the wind, P.Q. notes that the groaning continues even when the air is still. To the argument that the sounds might be an echo from the tree's hollow interior, "boring Instruments, Glister Pipes, &c.," P.Q. notes, prove that the tree is solid (P.Q., 1742: 6–7). In sum, the natural philosophical explanations P.Q. relays rely upon faulty observations and, as a consequence, are as inaccurate and inadequate as the explanations that evoke supernatural forces. P.Q.'s dismissals (whether supernatural or natural philosophical) underscore his status as an expert, and pave the way for his experimental practice and findings. His conclusion is reliable, he argues, because it is based on careful observation: "a long Series of Study" led to the discovery that the tree's sounds are in fact vibrations of its "ductile Organs and Alimentary Tubes" (P.Q., 1742: 7, 9).

Although presented with confidence, P.Q.'s explanation does not seem to be enough to prove conclusive, for he immediately calls upon the authority of the natural philosopher and physician George Cheyne. In *Essay on Regimen* (published in 1740, two years before *The Hampshire Wonder*), Cheyne develops ideas about "vegetable Matter" (in line with his by-then overt Platonism and Neoplatonism) to argue for the existence of "an infinite chain between matter and spirit" (Guerrini, 2000: xv). Therefore, when P.Q. concludes that *The Hampshire Wonder* is a tree animated by minute, imperceptible bits of divine presence, he cites Cheyne's theory of matter: "*Infinitesimal* Particle[s] of Celestial Matter" (Cheyne, 1740: 42). Perhaps ironically, P.Q.'s source text was the most poorly received of Cheyne's mature works; he had to pay his publisher £80 to buy back unsold sheets (Guerrini, 2000: 173). And at a minimum, P.Q. seems to exaggerate when claiming that Cheyne's theories are "now generally known and allowed" (P.Q., 1742: 8). Nevertheless, P.Q.'s explanation offers its natural philosophical fact as conclusive, in terms of inquiry, narrative, and authority, and as a resolution of the text's inaugural enigma.

When P.Q. promises to "clear up certain *Matters of Fact* relating to the Time and Manner of [the tree's] groaning," the text uses language associated with early natural philosophical discourse (P.Q., 1742: 6; emphasis added).

"*Matters of Fact*": various historians of science have taught us that "facts" emerged as a conceptual category to ground nascent natural philosophical practice. As such, facts were understood as reliable in no small part because they were available to scrutiny (Shapin and Schaffer, 1985: 80–154; Poovey, 1998: 92–143). However, as I have argued, if the idea of a "fact" at the heart of natural philosophical theory and practice was a key concept to legitimize the discipline, then it was manufactured through the combination of observable experience and literary, imaginative thinking (Chico, 2018: 32–42). To take the example of Robert Hooke's microscopic specimens, described and engraved in *Micrographia: Or Some Physiological Descriptions of Minute Bodies* (1665): although they are presented as single, singular objects – and thus, facts – they are in fact composites. Hooke's minute particulars of microscopy are the direct result of an imaginative process that sutures distinct examples. The representation of a natural philosophical fact might suggest that it is singular observation, but it is not. Instead, a natural philosophical fact simultaneously requires and obscures an imaginative process.

Others have also considered implications of these imaginative underpinnings animating early scientific theory and practice. For example, Helen Thompson sees this potential at work, in analogous ways, in empiricist philosophy and the novel: she asks, how may one conjure the insides and outsides of an object, whether for scientific or fictional ends? Thompson's insight is that both discourses imagine an encounter between subject and object, while also holding open the strong possibility that more lies beyond what one might sense (Thompson, 2017: 1–25). Robert Boyle's corpuscular chemistry, in particular, promotes an empiricism that stages a *sense* of the real through its figurations; operating on a similarly figurative register, therefore, is the quality of realness that eighteenth-novels dramatize.[4]

When P.Q. pledges to "clear up certain Matters of Fact," the text also seems to evoke the concept of the "modest witness" of earlier scholars (Shapin and Schaffer, 1985: 65–69; Haraway, 1997: 23–30) – that is, the individual who claims objectivity by erasing himself through his privilege. However, this, too, is a fiction. As I have argued, the identity of the "modest witness" requires figuration and imagination to reconfigure what is, in reality, an embodied experience (Chico, 2018: 35–75). I join other scholars who also consider such possibilities.[5] Thompson contends that the empirical observer is embodied (Thompson, 2017: 28–40) and Al Coppola posits that a mandate for performance gives shape to eighteenth-century natural philosophical inquiry which, as a consequence, eschews the masculinized modest witness in favor of a sentimental, feminized observer (Coppola, 2016: 145–77). More recently, Kristin M. Girten uses the figuration of "sensitive witnesses" to characterize seventeenth- and eighteenth-century women writers' argument that a human's closeness to nature, rather than one's alienation from it, leads to superior natural philosophical knowledge, a precedent that anticipates our modern-day "material feminism" (Girten, 2024: 14–15). In *The Hampshire Wonder* one can see this potential for an embodied viewer in the pamphlet's conclusion.[6] P.Q. speculates that some people are more likely to hear the tree's groans than others because the "infinitesimal Particle" of some human bodies is, like a string instrument adjusted to a standard pitch, "tuned to the infinitesimal Particle of the vegetable Body" (P.Q., 1742: 10). Others bodies are not.

Yet before P.Q. speculates about why only some people hear the tree, he presents his final natural philosophical explanation with the identical phrase,

---

[4] Jonathan Kramnick (2010), Jayne Elizabeth Lewis (2012), Wolfram Schmidgen (2013), and Courtney Weiss Smith (2016) also study representations that challenge the science-realism assumption in relation to fictionality, novelistic and poetic.

[5] Some view this possibility as only emerging later than I do. For example, Peter H. Reill argues that in the mid-eighteenth century, vitalism overtook mechanistic philosophy as a prevailing scientific model, a transformation that opened up the observer's newly intimate and entangled relation with the natural world (Reill, 2005: 33–70).

[6] My thanks to the anonymous reader for suggesting this possibility.

"infinitesimal particle." The term "Particle" evokes corpuscular chemistry, which Thompson instructs us is a paradigmatic exemplar of early empiricism because its "imperceptibility and perceptibility enable access to minuscule constituents of things" (Thompson, 2017: 2).

P.Q. relies upon not only Cheyne's ideas about vegetable matter but also on his language. The explanation for what causes the tree's groans opens with a direct quotation:

> And first I shall lay it down for a Rule, and I believe now generally known and allowed, * "That the *Infinitesimal* Particle of celestial Matter, that is, the *Miniature* of a *Miniature in infinitum*, decreasing in a continued *analogical* Progress, and stored up in the Seeds of all Animals and Vegetables, I say this divinely organized Vehicle or *Corpuscle*", (and I beg the Reader wou'd be very attentive to the Concatenation of my Argument) being stimulated by a Redundancy of vegetable Matter, operating on the ductile Organs and Alimentary Tubes, (viz. of the Tree) produces certain elastic Vibrations by its Protusion and the Extension of Plastic Nature, which Vibrations are the real Cause of those Singultus or Sobbings which the Vulgar call *Groaning*.
>
> * Vide Dr. *Cheyney*'s *Essay* on Regimen: Page 42. (P.Q., 1742: 8–9)

In a single sentence, P.Q. uses Cheyne's words to legitimize his own explanation. P.Q. first does this by transcribing Cheyne's use of the term "infinitesimal" and the elaboration of its meaning: "that is, the *Miniature* of a *Miniature in infinitum*." Just as Cheyne's figuration of infinitesimal posits a never-ending diminution, tinier and tinier and tinier, by mathematical definition, "infinitesimal" conveys something so small that it cannot be quantified: it is "a quantity less than any assignable quantity" (*OED*, 1989: s.v., 2.b.). By contrast, when Hooke needed to define (and defend) microscopic observations as reliable natural philosophical accounts of minute objects, he repeated the phrase "exceeding small": "*exceeding small Bodies*, or *exceeding small Pores*, or *exceeding small Motions*" (Hooke, 1665: Preface). "Exceeding small" is small, but perceptible with an optical instrument, the microscope. But Cheyne's and P.Q.'s concept of "infinitesimal" introduces a different ontological and epistemological challenge. Infinitesimal is an amount so small that it cannot be measured or perceived. Infinitesimal is also an amount so small – and this is key – that it cannot be known. An "infinitesimal particle" is something that can only be imagined. And just as unknowable as "Infinitesimal" is the term it modifies. Quoting Cheyne, P.Q. names "the *Infinitesimal* Particle of celestial Matter." The word "celestial" connotes the sky but always in the context of the divine: "celestial Matter" is *heavenly* matter. "Celestial Matter," too, exceeds sensory perception and thwarts knowability.

And "the *Infinitesimal* Particle of celestial Matter" is a form of matter only available to one's wonder.

P.Q.'s conclusion that undetectable heavenly matter echoes through the tree explicitly signals the need for the imagination: this is a natural phenomenon that cannot be measured, much less observed; only its effect (the groaning) can be apprehended and only by some. And yet rather than extinguishing wonder, this explanation perpetuates it.

The seeming peculiarity of *The Hampshire Wonder* is in fact its exemplarity: thick description of an unexplained natural phenomenon, vivid accounts of its effects on witnesses, and allusions to multiple explanations – the "unphilosophical notions" of a Mandrake, the antipodes, and a ghost; lore about an historical precedent; natural philosophical accounts that erroneously rely upon faulty observations; and P.Q.'s own natural philosophy that combines close observation of the tree with scientific theory concerning matter and spirit. With explanations taking up the majority of its pages, *The Hampshire Wonder* vividly demonstrates an important lesson: an encounter with a wonder is often inextricable from a desire to understand it.

3 Science's Wonder

For fifty years beginning in 1673, the Dutch naturalist Antoni van Leeuwenhoek, a minor city official in the Dutch town of Delft, wrote long, detailed letters to the Royal Society describing observations through his home-made single-lens microscope.[7] Accordingly, when Leeuwenhoek submits microscopical observations of a tongue to the Royal Society, he describes all he observes, including the papillae, which are "an unconceivable Number of painted Particles" (Leeuwenhoek, 1708: 114). This is a statement in which calculation fails, except, paradoxically, as a measure of the immeasurable. And in this moment of incalculability, using a technology of magnification that both reveals and produces wonder, Leeuwenhoek's report uses the term to characterize his observational practice. When he discovers new particles, it is "with great wonder" (Leeuwenhoek, 1708: 115). When he sees "a great Number of Holes or Cavities" in "several Scaley Particles," he writes, "I observed with wonder" (Leeuwenhoek, 1708: 117).

[7] Leeuwenhoek wrote in colloquial Dutch, Henry Oldenburg translated the letters, and others took over following Oldenburg's death in 1677, including Robert Hooke, who taught himself Dutch. The Royal Society commissioned Hooke and Nehemiah Grew, a botanist who was also appointed secretary, to replicate Leeuwenhoek's experiments (Schierbeek, 1959: 60, 34; Wilson, 1995, 88–90; Fournier, 1996: 75, 97; Ruestow, 1996: 146–200). Leeuwenhoek was elected a fellow of the Royal Society in 1680.

In the long eighteenth century, the concept of wonder profoundly shaped one of the period's most enduring legacies, natural philosophy, what today we understand as science. *The Hampshire Wonder*'s concluding endorsement of natural philosophy positions the discipline as both an outgrowth of and a response to wonder. This reflects an intellectual and cultural logic newly available in the long eighteenth century in which natural philosophy not only emerges from the multiple provocations of wonder but also finds its justification in wonder's astonishment, curiosity, and inquiry.

According to Katherine Park and Lorraine Daston, late seventeenth-century natural philosophers turned to "wonders" as objects of curiosity to study (Park and Daston, 1998: 215–54). While Park and Daston also argue that wonders as such fell out of favor shortly thereafter, wonder and wonders persist in natural philosophical discourse throughout the long eighteenth century. Take the example of Adam Smith's mid-eighteenth-century *The History of Astronomy*, which explicitly associates wonder and natural philosophy: "We wonder at all extraordinary and uncommon objects, at all the rarer phænomena of nature, at meteors, comets, eclipses, at singular plants and animals" (Smith, 1980: 34).[8] These "rarer phænomena of nature" are objects of study in natural philosophical disciplines – astronomy, botany, biology – and they likewise share the property of being, in Smith's language, "new" (Smith, 1980: 34). Extending the logic of this association, the exemplary individual who finds and responds to these objects is the natural philosopher who "examine[s] a singular plant, or a singular fossil" (Smith, 1980: 39).

The enduring association between early science and wonder in this period has captured other scholars' attention as well. Mary Baine Campbell (1999) documents global wonders newly available to the imagination of British writers and scientists who, in turn, use the speculative possibilities inherent to these objects to imagine science and fiction as distinct things; Stephen Greenblatt (1991) studies the so-called discovery literature of the Americas as promoting fictions of encounter and possession; and Richard Holmes (2008) characterizes the late eighteenth and early nineteenth centuries as "the age of wonder" in which science became popularized, proffering a story of discovery that upholds the mythologies of scientific and poetic genius.

What do I mean by science's wonder?

I take a cue from Ralph Bauer's recent insight that the notion of discovery of "America" (and, by extension, what others come to view as its various wonders) is a consequence of, rather than catalyst for, colonial conquest (Bauer, 2019).

[8] Smith probably wrote *The History of Astronomy* around 1748 and it was published posthumously in 1795 (Smith, 1980: 5–11).

Bauer teaches us that the Americas before the seventeenth century were not uniformly viewed by Europeans as new, strange, and unknown, but instead as sites of *other* people's knowledge. The idea of discovery was retrospectively written on to the cultures, landscapes, and potentials of the Americas, accomplished by the potent combination of conquest, law, and religion. Bauer's focus is not on wonder, or on wonder and science *per se*, but his analysis reminds us of the significance of these concepts as processes with durations and as entanglements of peoples, places, and things.

Natural philosophy's wonder not only activates feeling and a desire to know. It also stages relations between and among objects and subjects.

Wonder, for early natural philosophers, was currency: wonders provided the objects of study and wonder served up the entangled feelings of astonishment and intellectual curiosity.

The Royal Society of London for Improving Natural Knowledge, founded in 1660 and chartered in 1662, brought together various scientific groups of the interregnum (Hall and Hall, 1969: 157–68). Its meetings and publications were preoccupied by wonders and wonder. An issue from the 1667 *Philosophical Transactions* includes a two-page observation (the scientific genre) by Robert Boyle that describes a colt with no discernable nose, a single oversized eye, and a large growth on its forehead. Boyle's examination reveals that what appears to be a single eye is not but two eyes that share a single optic nerve, and that the fibrous tissue on the colt's forehead is nasal cartilage (Boyle, 1667: 86). Seventy years later, William Gregory, a surgeon, recounts operating to remove a pin-like object from the bladder of a baby born with "no Anus, neither privities to distinguish of what Sex it was" (Gregory, 1738: 368).

Alongside the Royal Society, numerous pamphlets, poems, ballads, lectures, demonstrations, and performances staged wonder and wonders for an eager audience. P.Q.'s pamphlet about the groaning tree, *The Hampshire Wonder*, is just one such example. Another is a 1701 broadside about the wonder of a young Dutch boy's eyes. Presented in the milieu of the London coffee house, the narrator advertises that a boy named Henrick T. Kent has in his right eye an inscription in "Latin, … in Capitals, *MEUS DEUS*" and "the same Words in Hebrew, *viz. ADONAI*" in the left (*Wonder of Nature*, 1701: 3). Readers are urged to go to "Mr Powels Coffee House near the Royal Exchange in Cornhil, where the Parents are ready to confirm every particular contained herein" (*Wonder of Nature*, 1701: 8). Having been trotted out and displayed around Holland and France, including a spell at court, the boy is now "daily seen" in the commercial heart of the City of London, observed "by Persons of the highest

Rank and Quality" who express "wonderful admiration and satisfaction, the like having not been known in the memory of Man" (*Wonder of Nature*, 1701: 6). Like a tiny Gulliver put on display as a curiosity in Brobdingnag, young Henrick T. Kent is an object of wonder guaranteed to produce the feeling of wonder – for a fee.

A perennial question with any object imagined as a wonder, and any experience of wonder, is, how to know whether something is, as it were, *real*? Within natural philosophical discourse and praxis, a primary mechanism for creating credibility, as Steven Shapin and Simon Schaffer taught us many years ago, hinged upon the notion of "virtual witnessing," that is, a collective agreement produced through the publication of experiments and demonstrations (Shapin and Schaffer, 1985: 22–79). In part as a result of this imperative, the textual archive of wonder and wonders is extensive.

Part of the Royal Society's vision was that anyone could contribute to the national project of building scientific knowledge. Thomas Sprat's *The History of the Royal Society of London*, for example, presents a collective that includes "the *Soldier*, the *Tradesman*, the *Merchant*, the *Scholar*, the *Gentleman*, the *Courtier*, the *Divine*, the *Presbyterian*, the *Papist*, the *Independent*" (Sprat, 1722: 427). Evoking an image of the city, Sprat sees the Royal Society "compounded of all Sorts of Men, of the *Gown*, of the *Sword*, of the *Shop*, of the *Field*, of the *Court*, of the *Sea*; all mutually assisting each other" (Sprat, 1722: 76). Indeed "social leveling" was a fundamental value of natural philosophy, even if this were not the case in practice (Hunter, 1982: 116, table 6). Although the membership fees would have been prohibitive for many but the most elite, the Royal Society did bring together people who would not have usually interacted socially (Hunter, 1982: 8; Shapiro, 2001: 309). Those who, in the words of Stephen Pumfrey, "did the work" were often of a lesser social rank, such as the lower born Robert Hooke (Pumfrey, 1995: 131–56).

Even with, or perhaps precisely because of, these models of membership, published observations and descriptions were expected to follow strict guidelines. The 1663 statutes governing the Royal Society detail that "In all Reports of Experiments to be brought into the Society, the matter of fact shall be barely stated, without any prefaces, apologies, or rhetorical flourishes; and entered so in the Register-book, by order of the Society" (*Record of the Royal Society*, 1940: 290). This requirement generated various technologies of verification, a common version of which was attestation. Gregory, the surgeon, concluded his contribution with a personal vow supplemented by the authority of witnesses: "I declare [this] to be Truth, having open'd the Child in the Presence of several Spectators. Witness my Hand, Wm. Gregory" (Gregory, 1738: 369). When a Dutch physician, Daniel de Superville, describes multiple "monstrous births," and speculates about their causes (for instance, blaming one on a mother's "disturbed and disordered Imagination"), he emphasizes the various honorifics that legitimize him. De Superville is "Privy Counsellor and chief Physician to his most Serene Highness the Margrave of Brandenburg-Bareith, President of the College of Physicians, Director of the Mines and of all Medicinal Affairs in the Margravite, Member of the Imperial Academy Naturae Curioforum, and of the royal Society of Berlin" (de Superville, 1740: 306). The anonymous author of the broadside about the little Dutch boy with writing in his eyes explicitly cites the authority of the intellectual and social elite, assuring readers that this is no fraud because a phalanx of "several eminent Divines, Doctors and other Learned Men" confirm the presence of the phrase "My God" in Latin and Hebrew (*Wonder of Nature*, 1701: 3–4). All of these accounts are typical in that they share an investment in cultivating the idea that a natural philosopher is best suited to study the wonders of nature – to study the wonders of nature, in this context, is also to adjudicate them.

Even an officer of the Royal Society was subject to and upheld the requirements of collective agreement. When Martin Lister (1638–1712), vice-president of the Royal Society and court physician, and best known as England's first arachnologist and conchologist, writes explicitly to convince his peers that he brings a worthy object of study, he invokes these various rationales. Of interest to Lister – and he argues, to the collective – is the wonder of "very aged Persons," centenarians and supercentenarians, anywhere from 100 to 140 years old. Lister's submission to *Philosophical Transactions* presents a *dramatis personae*: one Robert Montgomery, aged 126; a Mary Allison who died at 108; and a son and father, aged 100 and 140, respectively. Notably, Lister cautions his colleagues that "you must not take these Reports as Authentick and exact," and admits that "I find it a very hard, and troublesome business to verifie precisely the *Ages* of such Persons" (Lister, 1684: 597–98). Lister concedes that this might seem like a tall tale. But the point is – and this is key to his rhetorical and intellectual presentation – he is not *unconvinced*. Lister even speculates that their diet, which is "exceeding course, as salted and dryed Beef, and sower-leavened Oat bread," could be a root cause (Lister, 1684: 598). Lister ultimately relies upon the persuasive power of his own credibility and status: "I am confident many scores of persons might be found of the age of 100 years among these Northern Mountains," concluding that these reports are "credible enough, to make the matter worth the Examination" (Lister, 1684: 598). To meet the threshold for consideration, Lister's petition must list, caution, and ultimately affirm that the wonder of these "very aged people" in the north is a proper object for scientific inquiry. Rhetorically, Lister layers his own belief onto this wonder and, in so doing, taps into his standing among his peers.

These attestations of wonders contribute to a process that a French correspondent with the Royal Society characterizes as a "tribunal," a legal structure that gathers several representatives to adjudicate on behalf of a collective. In 1738, *Philosophical Transactions* published a letter sent by a Provençal nobleman, Joseph de Seytres, Marquis de Caumont, to Hans Slone, then president of the Royal Society. Caumont discusses an unusual stone or "calculus" extracted by a surgeon of the former's acquaintance from the bladder of a corpse that the authorities in France do not recognize. Caumont's compliments to Sloane and the Royal Society are extravagant: "The perfect Veneration I have for you" and "All *Europe* does Justice to your Merit" (Caumont, 1738: 370). But the specificity of the Marquis' praise also articulates a clear-eyed assessment of wonder's fundamental role in the pursuit of scientific knowledge: "You have an indisputable Right to all the Wonders of Nature: They have, in some manner, recourse to your Tribunal: For where can they be examined with such Judgment?" (Caumont, 1738: 369). Caumont's image of a "Tribunal" of wonder may directly specify the Royal Society. But more broadly, this "Tribunal" of wonder and wonders names both a corporate body and a process.

A case in point: natural philosophers were long fascinated and drawn to the idea of zoophytes. Although Linnean classification outlined the categories of rocks, plants, and animals (in 1758, Linnaeus published the 10th edition of *Systema Naturae*), widespread interest and discussion in the possibility of zoophytes continued well throughout the eighteenth century. In the Linnean system, exceptions illuminated the distinctions: coral, for example, is often understood as an organism that exists on the conceptual boundary between plant and animal. The "Tartar Lamb," also known as the "Vegetable Lamb," the "Scythian Lamb," and the "*Cibotium barometz*," seemed to be one of those exceptions.

Over a period of nearly one hundred years, the "Tartar Lamb" returned four times as an object of wonder and study to fellows of the Royal Society. And four times it was denounced.

1666. In August 1666, Sir Theodore de Vaux, physician to Charles II, read papers to the Royal Society from the Elizabethan ambassador to Russia, Sir Richard Lee, who claimed to have received one as a gift (*Journal Book of the Royal Society*, 1666: 2.232–33). The archival record documents that various observers were skeptical, including Francis Bacon in *Sylva sylvarum* (Bacon, 1857–74: 4.433), John Evelyn (Evelyn, 1825: 2.55–56), and Tsar Alexi's physician in Moscow, Samuel Collins, who called it a ruse in a letter to Boyle (Collins, 1671: 85).

1698. Then, over thirty years later, the Tartar Lamb again came under scrutiny when Hans Sloane published a repudiation of it in *Philosophical Transactions*. Referring to the adjacent engraving, Sloane opens without holding back, "*Fig. 5* represents what is commonly, but falsely, in *India*, called, *The Tartarian Lamb*," and continues with a detailed description:

> This was more than a Foot long, as big as ones Wrist, having several Protuberances, and towards the end some Foot-stalks about Three or Four Inches long, exactly like the Footstalks of Ferns, both without and within. Most part of the outside of this was cover'd with a Down of dark yellowish Snuff-Colour, shining like Silk, some of it a quarter of an Inch long. . . . It seem'd to be shap'd by Art to imitate a Lamb, the Roots or climbing part is made to resemble the Body, and the extant Footstalks the Legs. (Sloane, 1698: 461)

Sloane uses the language of similitude to disprove its veracity: this object "seem'd to be shap'd by Art to imitate a Lamb" (Sloane, 1698: 461). The agent of that artistry remains unnamed, an obfuscation amplified through the grammar of passive voice.

1725. The German-Polish botanist Johann Philipp Breyne ("Johannes Philippus Breynius") published his own account in 1725 of the Scythian lamb in *Philosophical Transactions* with an engraving of an even more lamb-like specimen. Breyne concludes that the object under consideration is either a root or stem that "had been skilfully manipulated into the form of a lamb" (Breynius, 1725: 353–60).

1750s. John Cook (who emigrated from Scotland to Russia in 1736, trained at the Medicine Chancery of St. Petersburg, worked as surgeon to Prince Mikhail Mikhailovich Golitsyn, and returned to Dundee in 1751) recalls that the Royal Society received and examined another specimen. It, too, was quickly confirmed as fraudulent: "within the skin, they discovered saw-dust or some other materials with which it was stuffed, and the navel pierced with a stick, which was so fixed, as to appearance, looked like a stalk" (Cook, 1997: 1.260–61). This mid-eighteenth-century Lamb of Tartar is a puppet-like contraption, rather than the much-hoped-for organic entity.

In each instance, the specific item was revealed as a hoax. Taken together, these instances suggest a lingering allure, a hope for the *possibility* that one might exist. They likewise indicate that the desire for something fundamentally impervious to the explanatory logics of natural philosophy seemed to call out for the explanatory logics of natural philosophy, time and time again.

Some so-called wonders like the Tartar Lamb kept being brought to the body's collective attention, even though they never achieved the status of a credible phenomenon and are, instead, discounted.

Some wonders, even when they fail to be wonders, never fully go away.

Some wonders persist as a specter of the unexplained and unknowable, as a sneaking suspicion, or even the just the hope, that something could both be true and be unknowable.

4 Wonder as Veneration

At the beginning of the seventeenth century, the notion that wonder might have a meaningful and productive relation to natural philosophical inquiry was, in Francis Bacon's view, unthinkable. Baconian empiricism, at the heart of the discipline's rationale, is at odds with the affordances of wonder. For Bacon, wonder is "nothing but contemplation broken off, or losing itself, . . . a tedious curiosity" (Bacon, 1857–74: 3.246). To feel wonder is solely an affective state, but – for Bacon – one that thwarts the potential for critical thinking that the concept comes to signify. The experience produces a subject who "ever breaketh off in wondering and not in knowing" (Bacon, 1857–74: 3.246). Baconian wonder is a self-propelling loop with no discernable route towards knowledge acquisition. Although Bacon concedes that "wonder is the seed of knowledge," following Platonic and Aristotelian thinking of wonder as the source of philosophy, he derides it as merely "an impression of pleasure in itself" (Bacon, 1857–74: 3.266). The following century, when David Hume discusses miracles in *Enquiries concerning Human Understanding and concerning the Principles of Morals*, which has typically been understood as his statement on revealed religion (Buckle, 2001: 239), he expresses concern that a miracle, or even a perceived miracle, might stimulate "the passion of surprise and wonder" and wonder, in particular, pushes one towards belief in no small part because it is "an agreeable emotion": "If the spirit of religion join itself to the love of wonder," Hume worries, "there is an end of common sense" (Hume, 1992: 117).

It was easy enough to mock natural philosophers as fools deluded by wonders and wonder, and many did. In the hands of contemporary satirists, natural philosophers' fascination easily, all too easily, leads to self-indulgence and self-delusion. Samuel Butler's "The Elephant in the Moon" (composed ca. 1676) imagines Royal Society fellows gathered around a telescope, fervently discussing lunar observations. Mistaken and ridiculous, they believe they witness an elephant on the moon, when in fact a small field mouse has gotten stuck in the telescope's lens, a circumstance that satirizes the "collective vision" promulgated by the Royal Society (Jarvis, 2016: 133–47). They are idiots, "who greedily pursue / Things that are rather wonderful than true" (Butler, 1973: p. 208, ll. 509–10). In Aphra Behn's *The Emperor of the Moon*, staged in 1687, the use of wonder to deceive is part of a plan, a trick concocted by young suitors to distract a patriarch-naturalist. The young men paint the slides of Dr. Baliardo's comically massive twenty-foot telescope, and he subsequently believes that he sees a royal court on the moon. Duped and suckered by his thirst for wonder, Dr. Baliardo is transfixed: his Baconian wonder, "impression of pleasure in itself," is the play's comedy and the source of his comeuppance (Bacon, 1857–74: 3.266). The bite of these satires comes from the fact that they highlight the ways that wonder as an experience shapes beliefs, truths, and a sense of what might be possible. The importance of collective agreement in the practice of natural philosophy includes the potential to be blinded by self-interest.

Of course, as we know, Bacon's skepticism yielded to the support of natural philosophers later in the seventeenth century. And as we have seen, natural philosophical texts about wonder and wonders proliferated. But questions remained. How might natural philosophical inquiry safeguard against the self-involved, self-aggrandizing fools that Butler and Behn ridicule? How might science's wonder be imagined as cultivating insight rather than foolishness, a sense of community rather than individualism? In addition to the production of knowledge, that is, what else does science's wonder produce?

Turning to the work of Robert Boyle offers some indications.

An Irish-Anglo gentleman, Boyle is best remembered as an influential natural philosopher, studying chemistry, physics, earth sciences, hydrostatics, medicine, alchemy, and natural history, and as a founder of the Royal Society. Known especially for discovering "Boyle's law" (also known as "Mariotte's law") – that is, the law that finds the pressure of a given amount of gas at a constant temperature varies inversely with its volume – Boyle was a prolific experimenter and a prolific author, publishing nearly fifty scientific works (Frank, Jr., 1980: 44). Boyle's lifelong focus on natural and experimental philosophy can be understood as a desire to make sense of observable, natural phenomena. In this capacity, Boyle ardently and vociferously denied that there was any imaginative or subjective aspect to the work, constructing a rhetoric and protocol of rigor to prove it. The man who argued against "rhetorical ornaments in setting down an experiment" (because that would be like painting the lens of a telescope, obscuring what one attempted to see) would seem to be an unlikely candidate for a discussion, much less an endorsement, of wonder (Boyle, 1661: 2.16).

However, in a text published six years before his death, *Of the High Veneration Man's Intellect Owes to God* (1685), Boyle focuses on wonder's centrality to natural philosophy: Boyle argues that wonder, whether as an object or an experience, naturally provokes scientific inquiry. Observation of "Corporeal things" leads to an experience of wonder, which, for Boyle, turns explicitly into the desire to *know* (Boyle, 1685: 94). Boyle is uninterested, say, in ghosts or miracles or other such things that might produce the feeling and experience of wonder and that might be called wonders. However, when expostulating that wonder is the source and occasion of natural philosophical inquiry, Boyle simultaneously attempts to preclude wonder's potential to manifest alternative intellectual hierarchies that have the potential, of course, to upset the tenets of the divine-human order. The danger, as Boyle imagines, is a forgetting of this spiritual hierarchy, a concern that opens *Of the Higher Veneration Man's Intellect Owes to God*. Boyle expresses "Indignation" that "many men, and some of them Divines, too, . . . presume to talk of Him and his Attributes as freely and unpremeditately, as if they were talking of a Geometrical figure, or a Mechanical Engine" (Boyle, 1685: 1). These "many men, and some of them Divines, too" are what Boyle elsewhere labels "sooty Empiricks," an adjective and noun combination that denigrates doubly as both foul and fraudulent (Clericuzio, 2010: 329–50). In the preface to the second part of his essay on niter, Boyle uses the phrase "sooty Empiricks" as a contrast to himself, within an apologetic statement about his own commitment to chemistry (Boyle, 1999–2000: 2.85). Boyle's *Of the Higher Veneration* indicts such free, spontaneous talk, "unpremeditated" in his phrasing, because discussions of the divine take on the tenor of scientific discussions. The "presumption and inconsiderateness of these men" means that knowing the former is rhetorically analogous to knowing the latter, an incommensurate parallel that Boyle contends verges on blasphemy (Boyle, 1685: 2). The similarity of rhetoric reveals, in Boyle's understanding, a similarity of epistemology that is not only inappropriate and inaccurate but also dangerous. Such free, spontaneous talk about God at once explicitly forgoes humility and implicitly promotes arrogance.

By comparing discussions of the divine to discussions of "a Geometrical figure, or a Mechanical Engine," Boyle seems to impugn natural philosophy, a praxis to which he is likewise committed.

Why?

With this peculiar analogy, Boyle lays the groundwork for the treatise's argument that wonder must be experienced in the service of a religious and social hierarchy. For Boyle, wonder may well be the spark that generates natural philosophical inquiry, but it also contains the potential to demean humans and to inflate the value of "Creatures . . . of a nature very much inferiour to ours" (Boyle, 1685: 94).

To avoid what he views as an inversion of the natural order that ought to place humans above animals, Boyle pivots to the indisputable (for him) hierarchy of the divine over the human: "the Divine Cause or Authour of them [natural phenomena] deserve[s] our Highest Wonder and Veneration" (Boyle, 1685: 2).

Contemplating, discussing, and aspiring to know God demands wonder, and yet this wonder for and about the divine must terminate in veneration, which is both a feeling and an action or fact. Veneration is, according to the *Oxford English Dictionary*, "a feeling of deep respect and reverence directed towards some person or thing" and "the action or fact of showing respect and reverence; the action or practice of venerating" (*OED*, 1989: s.v. 1 and 2). It positions the individual in an inferior relation to something else.

Boyle's pairing of "wonder and veneration" privileges rank and hierarchy. It also demands human submission and inferiority to the divine, in the process sharply clamping down on the potential for wonder to introduce and make available other forms of relations or alternative hierarchies. Although wary, Boyle does not renounce wonder, for the wonder one experiences examining the natural world must serve human veneration for and subjection to the divine. While the logic of binding wonder and veneration shows up, for instance, in Isaac Watts' use of admiration as a synonym for wonder (Watts, 1739: 17), Boyle's formulation explicitly configures wonder in the service of veneration: the collective focus of natural philosophers ought to be on "those Notices that are apt to increase their knowledge of God, and consequently their Veneration for Him" (Boyle, 1685: 86–87). With "the farther improvement of Telescopes," for example, the skies will yield "new Subjects for [astronomers'] wonder," including "new Constellations, and . . . new Stars, in those that are known to us already" (Boyle, 1685: 97). Telescopes therefore promise to sustain ever-growing scrutiny, offer more and more wonders, and provide ongoing occasions for the veneration of God. Scientific instruments work not only because they assist the observational process but also because they facilitate and ensure the individual's movement from wonder to veneration, ultimately framing scientific insight as a form of honoring the divine.

Boyle's trajectory from wonder to veneration appears well into the eighteenth century. When Charlotte Lennox explains in her mid-eighteenth-century periodical, *The Lady's Museum*, that in "the minutest animals we perceive the care and wisdom of an infinite power exerted for their formation and protection," she voices the view that careful observation of the natural world leads to a profound and humble appreciation of the divine (Lennox, 1760–61: 2.634). Seeing the wonders of nature is possible because of natural philosophy, but these things ultimately reflect the glory of God. In Lennox's exultation, "what an awe and adoration ought it to turn our thoughts towards the great Creator of them all!" (Lennox, 1760–61: 2.634). For John Dennis, astronomy is a vehicle to apprehend that "the more admirable Ideas and a more admirable Spirit . . . shew the attributes of the Creator" (Dennis, 1704: 53). Even studying debased and lowly worms culminates in "an Admiration of the Creator" (LeClerc, 1721:

dedication). In *The Spectator* no. 413, Joseph Addison argues that wonder, by design, inculcates the gloriousness of the divine: God "has annexed a secret Pleasure to the Idea of any thing that is new or uncommon, that he might encourage us in the Pursuit after Knowledge, and engage us to search into the Wonders of his Creation"; such pleasure "serves as a Motive to put us upon fresh discoveries" (Addison and Steele, 1965: 3.545). And Henry Baker urges readers to take up microscopy so as to "pass those leisure Hours agreeably and usefully in contemplating the wonders of the Creation, which otherwise would be spent in tiresome Idleness, or perhaps, some fashionable and expensive Vice" (Baker, 1742: 51).

Wonder as veneration is narrativized in Henry Jones's *Philosophy, A Poem, Addressed to the Young Ladies who Attended Mr. Booth's Lectures in Dublin* (1746), which imagines a scientific demonstration given by the Scottish itinerant lecturer John Booth. Throughout this period, lectures and demonstrations were staged in a variety of locales, including the Royal Society, coffee houses, shops, and private homes (Stewart, 1999: 133–53). In fact, after official meetings adjourned, fellows of the Royal Society continued their discussions in coffeehouse gatherings (*A Dissertation*, 1750: 9, 32–35). Jones' poet imagines the setting of Booth's lecture, commanding the audience of "young ladies" to visualize scientific instruments such as a prism and a magnet: "Behold ye Fair how radiant Colours glow" and "Lo! Here the Magnet's Magic charms the Sight, /And fills the Soul with Wonder and Delight" (Jones, 1746: 4). Following Boyle's model, the poem directs wonder into veneration, enjoining young women to study nature because it is "Fill'd with the Wonders of her Maker's Hand" (Jones, 1746: 7). The point is clear: natural philosophical examination might be generated by wonder, but it also must always use that wonder to promote the humility of faith.

And yet.

Wonder as veneration also introduces the possibility of its manipulation – wonder as control. An early optical instrument, the magic lantern, mobilizes this possibility.

A descendent of the camera obscura, the magic lantern projects images on a wall. It does so by means of a concave mirror positioned behind a candle with a lens in front. Much of the magic lantern's history could be said to be dedicated to producing the experience of wonder for viewers. For example, early designers sketched astounding slides for it – striking images that would appear, as if by magic, on a wall. In ten figures, "Death," Christiaan Huygens portrays a skeleton in motion (it walks, removes its head, and tosses the skull in the air) and Athanasius Kircher illustrates a magic lantern's projection of death with a scythe and an hour glass (Huygens, 1950: 197; Kircher, 1646: frontispiece). The Dutch mathematician Willem Jacob's Gravesande published a 1720 volume (translated into English by the popularizer, John Theophilus Desaguliers) with an engraving of the magic lantern projecting an image of a minotaur (Gravesande, 1731: 2.131). Other early champions were keen to harness the magic lantern's pedagogical potential. Gottfried Wilhelm Leibniz predicted that the magic lantern could be used to teach lessons on perspective and motion, Johann Zahn suggested projections for anatomical lessons, and Bonifacius Heinrich Ehrenberger made slides to accompany lectures on natural history, geography, and mathematics (Leibniz, 1675: n.p.; Zahn, 1702: 729–36; Ehrenberger, 1713: 1–22).

In late seventeenth-century England, Robert Hooke developed an interest in the magic lantern, publishing a paper in *Philosophical Transactions* (1688), in which he asserts the originality of his particular design.[9] While briefly suggesting that his version could be "of great use in painting," Hooke's attention primarily focuses on the magic lantern's capacity for tricking viewers (Hooke, 1668: 743). Its projections produce, in viewers, "Effects not only very delightful, but . . . [also] very wonderful" (Hooke, 1668: 741). His enthusiasm reminds us that magic lanterns could suggest an "inherent unruliness" (West, 2023: 115), even "paranoid projections" (Casid, 2015: 1–5). As an instrument, the magic lantern was always associated with "testing and shaping, even perverting, the limits of what could be imagined and believed" (Väliaho, 2022: 83). Hooke celebrates these possibilities when he describes the magic lantern's projections, which he notes, are vivid and credible enough that a viewer "would readily believe them to be super-natural and miraculous" (Hooke, 1668: 741). Under the spell of a magic lantern's images, Hooke predicts, viewers' affective experiences would come to encompass an ever-widening range of emotions, "all those passions of Love, Fear, Reverence, Honour, and Astonishment" (Hooke, 1668: 741).

Hooke's magic lantern tricks viewers. And for Hooke, this is the point.

Because the magic lantern provokes a comingling of feeling and belief, its images *seem* true and therefore enable the projector to manipulate an audience. The projections of Hooke's magic lantern initiate a process in which the presence of these feelings retrospectively institutes a belief in the veracity of the object that provoked those feelings.

[9] Hooke's language slides between an insistence upon "this Optical Experiment" being "New" and his qualification that he is merely suggesting modifications because it "hath not, that I know, been ever made by any other person this way" (Hooke, 1668: 741).

To promote his argument to the readers of *Philosophical Transactions*, Hooke presents a counterfactual history: "Had the *Heathen* Priests of old been acquainted with [the magic lantern], their Oracles and Temples would have been much more famous for the Miracles of their Imaginary Deities" (Hooke, 1668: 742). The scenario of "Heathen priests of old" presents a temporal and religious designation that distances the magic lantern from a contemporary usage, much less one a seventeenth-century natural philosopher would endorse. Even so, Hooke provocatively uses their example to illuminate the purpose of the magic lantern in his own day: within the pages of *Philosophical Transactions,* Hooke introduces and lauds the magic lantern as an instrument that divides viewers between those who know its secret and those who do not. In this regard, we learn, contemporaries are no different from those "Heathen priests of old" who would have (if they could have, that is) duped congregants. Hooke advises modern-day projectors to obfuscate so "that it may not be perceived by the Company in the room" and "the means how such Apparitions are made, shall not be discoverable" (Hooke, 1668: 742). Secrecy is necessary to ensure the success of the magic lantern, "the whole Operation" of which is to create these two audiences: those few who know its science and understand its mechanics as an instrument are distinct from, and implicitly superior to, those who are subjected to the wonder of its apparitions (Hooke, 1668: 743).

In contrast to the eighteenth-century *camera obscura*'s modeling of an individual's interiority, and long before the magic lantern's rise in the nineteenth century as the dominant visual technology (Park, 2023: 1–44), Hooke imagines using the magic lantern to institute social hierarchies and to control access to knowledge. Hooke's desire to use scientific instruments to manufacture wonder and, with it, a dumbfounded audience to control shows up in imaginative literature of the long eighteenth century. Margaret Cavendish imagines her empress subjecting an audience with wonder manufactured by technology in *The Description of a New World, called the Blazing World* (published in 1666) when she demands that "light" and "fire" chapels be constructed to enhance under her absolutist rule and religious authority (Cavendish, 2000: 193). The heroine of *The Female American* (published in 1767) discovers and uses a sun god sculpture megaphone to awe Indigenous peoples into adopting Christianity (*Female American*, 2014: 91–105). For Hooke, Cavendish, and the anonymous writer of *The Female American*, instruments produce wonder in order to awe and to control observers by sharply limiting who has access to learning how the technology works.

These writers dramatize that the potential to cultivate wonder in others is also, simultaneously and inextricably, the potential to exert mastery over others.

Hooke's stance on the magic lantern deviates sharply from his lifelong defense of scientific instruments. In his 1665 treatise, *Micrographia: or Some Physiological Descriptions of Minute Bodies*, one of the first two volumes published by the Royal Society, Hooke presents the case for the use of instruments in natural philosophical inquiry.[10] "Because [we previously] rely'd upon the strength of humane Reason alone," Hooke argues, "[we] have begun anew to correct all *Hypotheses* by sense" (Hooke, 1665: preface). Sensory perception, therefore, is improved by "Artificial Instruments" such as the microscope (and, by extension, other scientific technologies), which provide "a reparation made for the mischiefs, and imperfection, mankind has drawn upon it self" (Hooke, 1665: preface). Hooke's premise informs the justification of scientific instrumentation throughout the long eighteenth century – and beyond. Examples include John Floyer's "pulse watch," a pocket watch with a second hand to supplement (as in, improve by providing additional data) the physician's cutaneous perception as well as Hooke's own "rough scale," still in use today, that derives from "Hooke's law," in which force is proportional to extension (Hooke, 1678: 1–3; Floyer, 1707: 147–66).

In *Micrographia*, Hooke even imagines himself an instrument for others' use: "all my ambition is, that I may serve to the great Philosophers of this Age, as the makers of my Glasses did to me" (Hooke, 1665: preface). With this, we can apprehend a bit of the sleight of hand at play, reminding us of the myriad connections to the concept and practices of wonder and natural philosophy throughout the text. When a reader of *Micrographia* comes to the famous engraved plate of the flea, she must unfold it – a kinesthetic engagement with the material book that somatizes the wonder of a microscope's magnification. Accordingly, Frédérique Aït-Touati reads *Micrographia* as a wonder book (Aït-Touati, 2011: 144–48), in the literary tradition that David D. Hall adumbrates (Hall, 1989: 3–165), and Michael Hunter suggests that Hooke, while "a 'scientist' in a full, modern sense," was also "something of a 'wonder-monger'" (Hunter, 2003: 149).

If the microscope were associated with Hooke, then the airpump was with Boyle. Both were jewels of the early Royal Society, regularly brought out to show visitors (Hall, 1956: 185). Both also made phenomena invisible to the naked eye apprehensible.

Airpumps, of course, enabled the study of combustion and respiration, that is, qualities of *air*. When recounting experiments conducted in Oxford in *New Experiments Physico-mechanical, Touching the Spring of the Air, and its*

[10] The other volume published by the Royal Society was John Evelyn's *Sylva, or A Discourse of Forest-Trees and the Propagation of Timber in His Majesty's Dominions* (London, 1664).

Effects, Boyle characterizes air as a spring shaped like "a Fleece of Wooll" (Boyle, 1660: 165). The instrument of the airpump, Boyle emphasizes, does not distort natural phenomenon, nor does the individual operating it. He explains, "To proceed now to the Phaenomena, exhibited to us by the Engine above described; I hold it not unfit to begin with what does constantly and regularly offer it self to our observation, as depending upon the Fabrick of the Engine it self, and not upon the nature of this or that particular Experiment which 'tis employed to try" (Boyle, 1660: 20). Following this preamble, Boyle continues with the results, having assured his audience that the "Engine," that is, the airpump, "constantly and regularly offer[s] it self to our observation."

However, just as the microscope was notoriously difficult to use, so, too, was the airpump. It was also not necessarily reliable or trustworthy, as Boyle himself admits. In *A Defense of the Doctrine Touching the Spring and Weight of the Air* (1662), Boyle reports on experiments with the airpump designed to study Evangelista Torricelli's theory that vacuums come from atmospheric pressure, or in Boyle's words, the "Phaenomena of the Torricellian Experiment" (Boyle, 1662: 57). The treatise records experiments with the airpump to measure air pressure that ratify Boyle's "Doctrine of the Spring of the Air," the principle, now commonly known as Boyle's Law (the pressure of a mass of an ideal gas is inversely proportional to its volume at a constant temperature).[11]

Boyle is aware of the difficulties of experimentation. He discusses the problems one faces using an airpump, which include "the casual breaking of the Tube" (Boyle, 1662: 59). He also laments "the difficulty as well of procuring crooked Tubes fit for the purpose" (Boyle, 1662: 59). These conditions of the laboratory, as it were, these conditions of the materiality of the airpump, in turn prompt Boyle to offer a textual supplement. His experiments, he explains, may be accessed through "the ensuing Table," which he labels, "A Table of the Condensation of the Air" (Boyle, 1662: 60). In this table, Boyle transforms air into numbers, presented in rows and columns, to prove that the volume of a gas decreases as the pressure increases.

Although Boyle introduces the table as a supplement to the airpump experiments, within the text itself, the table is in fact a replacement. Glass tubes are ill-fitting and they break. But the abstraction of a table codifies as it distills. Whereas Hooke's magic lantern explicitly addresses the individual who manipulates it – particularly as someone who knows more than those who

[11] In 1660, Boyle included this theorem in his tract on the elasticity of air and, in response to a critic, published this *Defense* as an appendix to the second edition in 1662.

merely witness the effects – Boyle erases the presence of his experimenter, save for a "dexterous hand" (Boyle, 1662: 58).

What does Boyle's table suggest? If, for Hooke, Cavendish, and the anonymous writer of *The Female American*, instruments produce wonder in order to awe and to control observers in no small part by sharply limiting who has access to learning how the technology works, then how do we understand something as seemingly innocuous as Boyle's table that likewise sharply limits who has access to learning how the technology works?

Hooke's magic lantern is designed to trick. Is Boyle's table?

These writers – that is, Hooke, Cavedish, the anonymous author of *The Female American*, and even Boyle, too – dramatize that the potential to cultivate wonder in others is also, simultaneously and inextricably, the potential to exert mastery over others.

5 Wonder's Science

In 1713, John Whalley, a "Professor of Astrology and Physicks," published a pamphlet concerning the appearance of a "bleeding moon in the Dublin sky" on Sunday, 24 May, viewed "between ten and eleven at night" (Whalley, 1713: title page). The pamphlet follows a familiar narrative arc: Whalley presents reports of a seemingly wondrous natural phenomenon to explain in scientific terms what had seemed as inexplicable. Whalley concludes that what was observed in the sky the night in question was, in fact, an optical illusion called "a mock-moon" (Whalley, 1713: 7). However, the explanations of astronomy and physics cannot completely erase the possibility that the glowing moon in the Dublin sky is also a portent, evoking the tradition of interpreting wonders as political evidence (Curry, 1989; Burns, 2002). In Whalley's own language, he ascribes intellectual certainty to the miraculous with the phrase "It cannot be denyed" that such images in the sky "have constantly been Signs and Forerunners of Uncommon and strange Revolutions and Accidents (yea sometimes of even the most stupendious, in respect to the general Affairs of the World)" (Whalley, 1713: 5). Whalley calls readers to measure "whether we have not the greatest reason to look upon these Mock-Moons as *Trumpets* sent to *Awaken* and *Alarm* us to a more strict and thorough Inquiry into our selves and our present State, and to let everyone to amend one, and as much as possible contribute to that of his Neighbours and Country" (Whalley, 1713: 5).

If the red moon over Dublin is a quirk of the stars that can be explained by astronomy, then it is also a prodigy, a divine warning for humans to behave better. The former does not disprove or eradicate the significance and meaning of the latter, for more than one explanation, more than one episteme, may be valid concurrently. Whether identified as a bleeding moon or a mock moon, the phenomenon is at once a scientific fact and an otherworldly harbinger, two distinct yet equally plausible conclusions that draw upon distinct, seemingly contradictory explanatory regimes.

By holding up a supernatural explanation as equally valid as an astronomical one, Whalley urges readers to maintain the possibility that both are true. When Whalley presents these two incommensurate paradigms for understanding the moon as equally valid, he reflects the capaciousness of what "wonder's science" might be.

What is "wonder's science"?

To return to Boyle briefly: when Boyle posits channeling science's wonder into veneration, what results is an active and ongoing process with the potential to reorient time and space. This is what I call "wonder's science." Elaborating the significance of veneration and the imperative that wonder be directed to it, Boyle presents the divine as infinitude and one's attempts to study it requiring endless dynamism. Even though Boyle decries those "sooty Empiricks" for treating their study of God as like their study of geometry or mechanics, as we saw earlier, he relies upon a figuration from mathematics to convey veneration as a verb. And veneration for Boyle is like a form of transportation: "the Wonderfull Excellency of God" embodies (a term I use with some irony) infinitude: "how much soever one takes, there still remains more to be taken" (Boyle, 1685: 97). Calling forth in the reader's imagination "an infinite Series or row of ascending numbers," Boyle notes that though one can go "farther and farther," the line never ends (Boyle, 1685: 97). As one approaches, more numbers emerge at the horizon, akin to the study of "progressions in Infinitum" (Boyle, 1685: 97). Boyle imagines veneration as an *approach* – stretching towards something that can never be reached, straining towards something that continuously expands. And this *approach*, in the context of a landscape and a time that seem to unfold before our eyes – this *approach* characterizes wonder's science.

Eighteenth-century landscapes seem to be replete with wonder's science, particularly as reflected in the genres of the georgic and natural history. And those wonders and the wonder that results point towards a horizon far beyond the time and space of the present, enacting that *approach* in the process.

In the hands of John Dyer in his four-book georgic *The Fleece* (1757), wonder's science transforms sheep's fleece into the Navy's fleets, a multilayered metamorphosis of bleating sheep in the English countryside into woolen cloth exported around the world, traffic simultaneous with Dyer's celebration of

British naval capacity and commerce. If Dyer "overwhelm[s] the paradisal connotations of the Miltonic blank verse," as Karen O'Brien notes (O'Brien, 1999: 171), then this is accomplished through the logics of wonder's science. The sheep, fleece, and fleets coexist as "they": "How widely round the globe they are dispers'd, / . . . they speed their way" (Dyer, 1757: III.559, 562). This perspective reorients space and time, a feat that converts fleece into a commodity, labor into trade, the local into the global, the present animal into future profits. When *The Fleece* concludes by reimagining British trade as fundamental to life writ large, it is with an allusion to the science of pneumatics: "Britain's happy trade now spreading wide, / Wide as the' Atlantic and Pacific seas, / Or as air's vital fluid o'er the globe" (Dyer, 1757: IV.694–696). To an ear today, this phrasing might sound peculiar, but Dyer's description alludes to the pneumatic definition of air as fluid. In Robert Boyle's *The General History of Air* (1692), air is "that thin, fluid, diaphanous, compressible and dilatable Body, in which we breathe and wherein we move" (Boyle, 1692: 1). Wool as air does not merely resound on the figuration of air as a liquid but also conjures the association between wool and air that Boyle famously forged in *New Experiments Physico-Mechanicall, Touching the Spring of the Air, and Its Effects* (Boyle, 1660: 165). Boyle wrote at length about his search for the proper metaphor to describe the buoyancy and curvature of air, finally settling on wool. One hundred years later, Dyer draws on Boyle's signature wool metaphor as a way to claim that British trade is omnipresent, just like the air we breathe. In so doing, Dyer also draws upon wonder's science.

The diurnal, natural world – the landscape of English poetic form – also offers natural historians ample opportunity to reflect and develop wonder's science. As a genre, natural histories present copious and detailed scientific observations about plants and animals alongside myriad vignettes of wonder and the experience of wonder. Derbyshire's Peak District, according to a 1729 natural history, is "a Place composed of Wonders" (Martyn, 1729: 22). Gilbert White (2013) suffuses *The Natural History of Selborne* (published in 1789) with wonder's science. Here is a countryside populated by wonders that capture White's attention. Styled as letters to fellow naturalists, *The Natural History of Selborne* focuses on the limited geography of a rural Hampshire parish over a period of more than twenty years. (During the COVID-19 lockdown, Gilbert White's House & Gardens established a themed activity inspired by White's methodology, calling it "watching narrowly" [Weston, 2023].)

Birds, in particular, enthrall White. They ecologically reshape, Dustin D. Stewart has recently argued, what belonging to a parish might mean. White followed his favorite birds and, as a consequence, "creatively remapped local space . . . no matter how far [the favorite birds] traveled" (Stewart, 2023: 27). White reconfigures geography, demarcating a human-oriented social and religious space – the parish – according to aviary migration patterns.

And the bird in eighteenth-century natural history is always more than a bird, often enfolding various conceptual relations. In their writing of an eighteenth-century it-narrative, "Invention: The Raven and the Bobolink: An American Fable," Chi-ming Yang and Sarah Rivett demonstrate that natural history discloses links between early science, American nation building, and capitalism (Yang and Rivett, 2021). And through a singular focus on the bobolink (as a natural philosophical object) and its migrations afforded by Indigenous rice and Black labor and performance, Yang also teaches us that plantation capitalism creates crops and bird flight patterns, as well as opportunities for a critic's "experimental ekphrasis essay" (Yang, 2021: 87).

White's birds offer occasions for potentially radical reconsiderations of the familiar coordinates of observation, foregrounding the methodology and ethos of approach that characterize wonder's science. The Caprimulgus, variously called the goat-sucker, the churn-owl, and (now) the nightjar, is a favorite: "There is no bird, I believe, whose manners I have studied more" (White, 2013: 49). Its song fascinates White. The Caprimulgus occasionally "chatter[s] as it flies," but generally vocalizes while at rest, its head bowed (White, 2013: 49, 51). The bird "is most punctual" with its singing, "in beginning its song exactly at the close of the day; so exactly that I have known it strike up more than once or twice just at the report of the Portsmouth evening gun, which we can hear when the weather is still" (White, 2013: 51).

To describe the song of the Caprimulgus, White uses language of astonishment. It is a "jarring note" (White, 2013: 49). This phrase registers the initial affective experience of wonder. The text proceeds to study what causes the strength and physicality of the little bird's vocalizations, with White assuring readers that it is "past all doubt" that the bird's "notes are formed by organic impulse, by the parts of its windpipe, formed for sound" (White, 2013: 51); this, he explains, is similar to a cat purring.

However, the natural philosophical explanation does not conclude White's discussion nor, more notably, does it resolve his wonder. White subsequently tells a tale about the effect of the bird's vocalization on a group of friends who join him for tea. They gathered in an hermitage – a secluded, wooden, thatched building used as a summerhouse (White, 2013: 279, n. 51). When a Caprimulgus rested on "the cross of that little straw edifice and began to chatter," White recounts, "we were all struck with wonder to find that the organs of that little animal, when put in motion, gave a sensible vibration to the whole building!" (White, 2013: 51). White provides a natural philosophical explanation ("past all doubt") to explain the natural phenomenon they all witness. The bird's windpipe is shaped in such a way as to produce its singular song.

And yet: they wonder.

For Whalley and White, wonder continues alongside scientific explanation in an ongoing process. For others, natural philosophical practice itself has the potential to transform into a perpetual experience of wonder. Both options influence and co-exist in James Thomson's *The Seasons* (published in 1730), famously a poetic celebration of Newtonianism. In the verdant pastoral landscape of *Spring*, the character "Newton" appears just as a rainbow emerges in the sky. Newton is "awful," suggesting that he both embodies wonder and induces it in others (Thomson, 1981: *Spring* l. 208). And the rainbow itself is a "grand ethereal bow" "bestriding earth" that "Shoots up immense; and every hue unfolds" (Thomson, 1981: *Spring* ll. 204, 205).

However, addressing the character "Newton," Thomson's poet calls the rainbow "thy showery prism," explicitly evoking Newton's famous optical instrument and doing so with the intimacy of direct address and a possessive pronoun (Thomson, 1981: *Spring* l. 209). In the phrase "thy showery prism," the wonder of a rainbow as a natural phenomenon is supplanted by the wonder of Newton's optical discovery that white light, when refracted, breaks down into a rainbow of colors. Newton's transformation of a wonder (the rainbow) into a scientific fact (the refraction of light) itself produces a subsequent experience of wonder. Here, wonder does not merely linger; it infuses natural philosophical practice altogether. Thomson's Newton, god-like, commands nature: under his "sage-instructed eye," the rainbow "unfold[s] / The various twine of light" that are "by thee [Newton] disclosed" from "the white mingling maze" (Thomson, 1981: *Spring* ll. 209–11). For Thomson in *The Seasons*, Newtonianism produces wonder. In the case of the Newton figure, the poem accomplishes an intellectual sleight of hand: the transformation of a rainbow into "thy showery prism" encourages readers to view the wonders of the natural world not only through the lens of natural philosophy but also, with a more radical implication, as a consequence of that natural philosophy. The entity that produces wonder is not nature so much as the historical man.

Voltaire dispatches readers on a similar journey in a dedicatory poem to Émilie du Châtelet, the first French translator of *Principia*. Prefaced to *The Elements of Sir Isaac Newton's Philosophy* (translated by John Hanna into English in 1738), Voltaire's poem also uses the character of Newton to instruct readers in wonder's science. Just as Thomson's rainbow bends to Newton's will in *The Seasons*, the sea, comets, the moon, and the earth animate themselves for Voltaire's Newton, whom they celebrate as a "wond'rous Man" (Voltaire, 1738: l. 62). Voltaire personifies Newtonian natural philosophy as the "all-charming, pow'rful Queen, / [who] Lifts the wise Mind above corroding Spleen" to a plane "on high, where *Newton* now remains" (Voltaire, 1738: ll. 21–22). This is an intellectual and a physical place, a "vast Expanse" and a "Space, which contains th'Infinity of God" – and Newton (Voltaire, 1738: l. 34). Voltaire's poet takes readers to a region where only "Newton's Compass" can measure the seemingly immeasurable "soul of nature" (Voltaire, 1738: ll. 45, 43). "Newton's Compass" is an instrument beyond human scope and apprehension. The spatial plane that Voltaire's Newton both occupies and represents requires that the reader imagine the human in an unbounded, never-ending cosmos. As a consequence, what we experience is "so wondrous to our Sense" that it calls into question the ordinary markers of orientation (Voltaire, 1738: l. 37). To apprehend a minute particular, for instance, requires seeing it through two different scales of measurement simultaneously: both as a distinct, miniscule entity and as a mass undifferentiated from the expansive horizon in which it is entangled. The juxtaposition of scale intermingles the oppositional views of microscopy and telescopy: it is "an Atom in th'Immense" (Voltaire, 1738: l. 38). Voltaire creates a landscape that teaches the reader to see planes and dimensions apprehensible only through the coordinated work of observing and imagining.

Thomson's Newton, on the other hand, is not alone in *The Seasons*.

Fast on the luminary's heels, in hot pursuit of the wonder of the rainbow, a swain runs into the poem: he "wondering views the bright enchantment bend" – that is, the rainbow – "Delightful, o'er the radiant fields" (Thomson, 1981: *Spring* ll. 213–14). The swain's rainbow is not Newton's "showery prism," but a "bright enchantment." The placement of the swain's entrance in the poem jars, bursting forth in a spondaic fourth foot that interrupts Newton. The poet introduces the swain with a declaration of rejection: if the rainbow bows to Newton, "Not so the swain" (Thomson, 1981: *Spring* l. 212). The swain remains, in all ways, Newton's opposite. From the swain's perspective, the rainbow does not affirm Newtonian optics nor does it augur the mastery of natural philosophy over nature. Instead, for the swain, the rainbow's glorious colors are a "bright enchantment" that mirror, and amplify, the landscape's spring beauty. The swain and, by implication, the poem's reader perceive this pastoral topography through eyes and ears: "Moist, bright, and green, the landscape laughs around"; the countryside's "music wakes/ Mixed in wild concert," with "warbling brooks" and "bleatings of the hills" (Thomson,

1981: *Spring* ll. 197, 198–200). Whereas awful Newton looms and commands above all, the swain's wonder is desire, literalized by the act of running across the fields "to catch the falling glory" (Thomson, 1981: *Spring* l. 215). The swain's wonder never ends: even when the rainbow "vanish[es] quite away," the youth remains "amazed" and "Beholds th' amusive arch before him fly" (Thomson, 1981: *Spring* ll. 215–17). The figure of Thomson's swain embodies wonder's science – the desire to know is ongoing, a never-ending approach.

One could read the swain as deluded, of course, a Baconian fool swept up in wondering compared to the sober and all-knowing Newton. However, recall Thomson's placement of the swain: he interrupts the portrait of Newton, introduced by a statement of negation in a spondee, without even the breathing room of a line break from one to the next. The poem's metrics raise the possibility that the swain is as important to the logics of *The Seasons* as Newton is: by introducing the swain cheek-in-jowl with the character of Newton, the poem could be said to reframe its Newtonianism, balancing it with the swain who hopes to capture the rainbow only to see it elude him. Even if the poem's inclusion of the swain does not ultimately overturn *The Season*'s overall celebration of Newton as historical personage and intellectual lion, then one must still reckon with him, a youth embraced by and embracing of the wonders in the country landscape around him.

With this pairing, the poem not only keeps two possibilities afloat but also renders them inextricable. Thomson's poet lauds the wonder of natural philosophical genius, rendering scientific understanding as even more of a wonder than the natural phenomena it explains. Thomson's poet also lauds the swain's wonder defined by an endless seeking of that which lies just beyond the horizon, suggesting that an individual's wonder at a natural phenomenon might not, and perhaps even *should* not, end because there might be a scientific explanation for it. Wonder's science creates possibilities. Put into action, as we shall see in the following chapters, those possibilities include new forms of space and of time.

6 To Know with Wonder

In *The History of Astronomy*, Smith imagines the first time a person witnessed a magnet in action, that is, observing a metal object moving, seemingly on its own, towards another object. In Smith's rendering, this is a piece of iron drawn towards a lodestone "without any visible impulse" from the latter:

> the motion of a small piece of iron along a plain table is in itself no extraordinary object, yet the person who first saw it began, without any visible impulse, in consequence of the motion of a lodestone at some little distance from it, could not behold it without the most extreme Surprise; and

> when that momentary emotion was over, he would still wonder how it came to be conjoined to an event which, according to the ordinary train of thoughts, he could have so little suspect it to have any connection. (Smith, 1980: 40)

In the "now" of the telling, Smith concedes that seeing a magnet is hardly "extraordinary," yet he conjures a scenario requiring the reader to imagine the *first* person to witness this and, additionally, to imagine that person's experience of wonder. Henry Jones, as we recall, urged modern-day viewers and readers to see "the Magnet's Magic" (Jones, 1746: 4). Smith, however, creates a fictional and generalized time of the original witnessing, the individual would undergo two responses. The first would be "the most extreme Surprise." The second would be to think about how this happened and what caused it. In other words, the affective response of wonder, in this imagined viewer, is a "momentary emotion" succeeded by the more lasting quality of wonder as intellectual questioning. Smith's vignette renders both verbal connotations of wonder – as affective and as thinking. Reading *The History of Astronomy*, one may well agree with Alexander Dick's observation that Smith presents wonder as both a process of scientific inquiry, "from naïve wonder to established fact," and a subjective experience (Dick, 2019: 240).

But why does Smith choose the example of the first person observing a lodestone's magnetic pulling of iron to characterize wonder?

He does so to invoke Cartesian physics:

> When, with Des Cartes, we imagine certain invisible effluvia to circulate round one of them, and by their repeated impulses to impel the other, both to move towards it, and to follow its motion, we fill up the interval betwixt them, we join them together by a sort of bridge, and thus take off that hesitation and difficulty which the imagination felt in passing from one to the other. (Smith, 1980: 42)

Although the reader today is familiar with the phenomenon of magnets, to understand why they work we need to imagine, in Smith's words, "with Des Cartes." The human eye cannot perceive those "certain invisible effluvia" that "circulate round" the lodestone, only their effect on the iron. And that movement implies, but does not confirm, the existence of "intermediate, though invisible events," which are knowable only by imagining the work of René Descartes. Those "intermediate, though invisible events" persist as invisible and assumed. To the extent that this is possible, they are known through an imagination that simultaneously takes up the possibilities of Cartesian physics and interprets the kinetic effect of one material body on another.

To describe wonder, Smith explicitly alludes to Cartesian physics. His description also implicitly alludes to Cartesian wonder.

"When, with Des Cartes, we imagine."

In *The Passions of the Soul* (published in 1649 as *Les Passions de l'âme*), his final treatise, Descartes identifies the first passion as "l'admiration," translated into English as "wonder." Distinguished from the excesses of astonishment, Cartesian wonder is associated with novelty, for instance when we encounter something "new, or very different from what we have previously experienced or from what we expected it to be" (Descartes, 2015: §§ 53). Wonder has no opposite "because, if the object that presents itself has nothing in itself to surprise us, we are not moved by it in any way and we consider it without any passion" (Descartes, 2015: §§ 53). But key to Cartesian wonder is its operation as an intellectual activity: in the experience of wonder, "the soul is suddenly taken by surprise, which causes it to consider attentively the objects it finds rare and extraordinary" (Descartes, 2015: §§ 70). Wonder is not merely a feeling of astonishment and surprise at something new. It is also a form of study – wonder as thinking.

Whereas Bacon impugns wonder as producing broken, fragmented, and tedious thought, Descartes argues that wonder is a cognitive passion that trains the mind to think well. As Tili Boon Cuillé explains, Cartesian wonder "affects the mind, not the heart" (Cuillé, 2021: 30). Cartesian wonder focuses the mind and ensures that one *learns* and *remembers*: "we can say of wonderment that its particular utility is to enable us to learn and retain in our memory things of which we were formerly unaware" (Descartes, 2015: §§ 75). This is a distinctly *epistemological* experience: the passion of wonder is intellectual.

Nearly a century later, Isaac Watts, the dissenting minister, like his contemporaries, finds easy companionship in wonder and natural philosophy. In *The Doctrine of the Passions*, a wonder is "*rare* and *uncommon*, . . . *strange*, either for its Kinds, or for its Qualities" (Watts, 1739: 17). As a consequence, one experiences the passion of wonder "at a very great or a very little Man, a Dwarf or a Giant; at a very little Horse, at a huge Snake or Toad, at an Elephant, or a Whale, or a Comet, . . . at artificial Trifles, as a Flea kept alive in a Chain; at any uncommon Appearances in Nature discovered by a Telescope, a Microscope, &c." (Watts, 1739: 17–18). For Watts, as for Descartes, wonder is the first passion and is singular with "no opposite" (Watts, 1739: 18); even though its antithesis is neglect, neglect does not reach the threshold of being a passion (Watts, 1739: 19). For Watts, as for Descartes, wonder's function "is to fix our Attention upon the admired Object, to impress it more effectually upon our Memory" (Watts, 1739: 19).

Cartesian wonder requires attention and focus. Cartesian wonder is sustained intellectual engagement.

Cartesian wonder is "to know with wonder."

"When, with Des Cartes, we imagine."

As exemplified through the example of the iron and the lodestone, wonder, for Smith, first emerges at the moment one perceives difference. Smith describes this as when the mind fails to perceive a "smooth, and natural, and easy" connection between two objects (Smith, 1980: 39). Accordingly, the "imagination and memory exert themselves to no purpose," "fluctuat[ing] to no purpose from thought to thought, and we remain still uncertain and undetermined where to place it, or what to think of it" (Smith, 1980: 39). Sometimes, this uncertainty ends, in which case wonder ends, too. Other times, wonder persists if the mind determines that something only holds a faint connection to other things: if so, then "wonder is indeed diminished, but not quite destroyed" (Smith, 1980: 39).

By locating the perception of difference as the inaugural experience of wonder, Smith, too, reserves the possibility that such difference may remain unreconciled and, correspondingly, that the experience of wonder may extend interminably: "If we can recollect none, but are quite at a loss, it is the greatest possible [wonder]" (Smith, 1980: 39). If, in other words, a mind concludes that a thing is unlike anything else, then the mind's experience is wholly one of wonder.

To know with wonder, therefore, is a form of cognition in which an unreconciled difference might endure rather than collapse under pressures of similitude. Smith explains:

> The stop which is thereby given to the career of the imagination, the difficulty which it finds in passing along such disjointed objects, and the feeling of something like a gap or interval betwixt them, constitute the whole essence of this emotion. (Smith, 1980: 42)

Smith grants that wonder produces an affective experience in the body, leading to a "rolling of the eyes," the "suspension of the breath," and the "swelling of the heart" (Smith, 1980: 40–41). Watts holds on to a similar point: one is "struck" by it" "on a sudden, or in an unexpected Moment" or "to a high Degree" (Watts, 1739: 17–18).

Yet the "whole essence of this emotion," Smith contends, is captured by "the stop," "the difficulty," and "the feeling of something like a gap or interval."

For Smith, wonder is the state of the mind searching, seeking, trying to make sense. In the experience of ordinary thought, the mind brings things together; in a state of wonder, the mind still brings things together, but it must do so by imagining new relations. To know with wonder, the mind "endeavours to find out *something* which may fill up the gap, which like a bridge, may so far at least unite those seemingly distant objects" (Smith, 1980: 44; emphasis added).

Something – the term resists figuration and specificity.

Something – simultaneously nothing because it is imaginary *and* everything because it unites seemingly unrelated objects. When Emily Ogden writes about "not knowing," she captures possibilities that Smith foregrounds: "not knowing" is "a capacity to hold the position of not knowing yet – the possibility of not knowing ever. I'm talking about living with the dimness that I will mostly inhabit" (Ogden, 2022: 6).

Smith's wonder encompasses the verb as both an emotional experience and an intellectual one. Wonder is being surprised to see a lodestone pull a piece of iron. But wonder is also imagining what it means "to know with wonder," to envisage the approach – seeing in the mind's eye the Cartesian effluvia that causes one object to move towards the other. Smith's evocation of Cartesian physics in this paradigmatic moment of wonder teaches us that our minds can see relations between objects that are beyond ordinary sensory perception.

Smith's evocation of Cartesian physics also points us to Cartesian wonder. The knowing of wonder is not only the conjunction of observation and imagination but also a mode of apprehension and cognition that thinks through science to conjure a world where space and time can be reimagined, where their fullness and amplitude open up other possibilities.

John Arbuthnot's poem, *ΓΝΩΘΙ ΣΕΑΥΤΟΝ, Know Your Self: A Poem* (1734), takes up the possibility of thinking with science. As I discuss in the beginning of this Element, Arbuthnot refuses to think of himself as reduced to a mass of veins and blood. He also contemplates viewing the universe through Pascal's physics. Arbuthnot begins with imagining through telescopic technology: "Now with swift Thought I range from Pole to Pole / View Worlds around their flaming Centers roll" and then "I trace the blazing Comet's fiery Trail, / And weigh the whirling Planets in a Scale" (Arbuthnot, 1734: 3). It is not the eye that "ranges from Pole to Pole," but the speaker's "swift Thought." Such sights of the cosmos are, for Arbuthnot, "Godlike Thoughts" that seem to raise the speaker to another plane of existence (Arbuthnot, 1734: 3). And imagine Arbuthnot writing now, if you will, thinking with the recent astronomical discovery that space is choppy and that it churns, the result of a measurable, "gravitational wave background" – predicted by Einstein nearly a century ago (Agazie et al., 2023: 1).

However, Arbuthnot's residency in this airy, beyond-the-human realm is short-lived, punctured by the introduction of another paradigmatic form of natural philosophical observation, microscopy. The gnat, the discipline's telltale specimen, catches the speaker's eye and mind, and provokes a form of degradation simultaneously physical and conceptual: "Some glitt'ring Trifle offer'd to my view, / A Gnat, an Insect, of the meanest kind, / Erase the new-born Image from my Mind" (Arbuthnot, 1734: 3). When Arbuthnot modifies the baseness of an insect, "the meanest kind," with the adjective "glitt'ring," the speaker evokes the transformative properties of natural philosophy, which can see beauty in the abject. However, for Arbuthnot, thinking with natural philosophy offers the promise to "know your self," but it does not deliver, as I note earlier: "This Frame, . . . I call it Mine, not Me" (Arbuthnot, 1734: 2).

While Arbuthnot's poem takes up, only to reject, the imaginative possibilities afforded by natural philosophy, Elizabeth Carter's 1738 verse, "While clear the Night, and ev'ry Thought serene," likewise dedicated to contemplation of the sky, does so through the knowing with wonder that Smith later articulates. Carter's poem opens with an invitation for the reader to ascend to the sky, accomplishing the journey as an act of imagination: "Let Fancy wander o'er the solemn Scene: / And, wing'd by active Contemplation, rise / Amidst the radiant Wonders of the skies" (Carter, 1999: ll. 1–3). "The skies," Carter's spatial destination for the reader, hosts "radiant Wonders." By linking wonder as a noun to an adjective of illumination, Carter offers a figurative analogue to the sparkling lights brightening the night sky. In fewer than the two dozen lines of the poem, we encounter a collection of synonyms for "radiant," itself adjectively connected to "Wonders": "blaze," "Beams," "gilds," "Light," "illumes," "radiant," "shines," "ray," "blaze," "glimmers," "twinkling" (Carter, 1999: ll. 6, 9, 13, 14, 15, 16, 18, 19, 20, 21, 22). With the command that the reader "Let Fancy wander," Carter employs a near homonym, "wander" for "wonder" and, in the process, animates wonder as a verb of movement, reminiscent of Thomson's swain. But Carter's "radiant Wonders" are available to a fancy that wanders and that wonders, buoyed by the sort of expansive and imaginative thinking that converts a noun into a verb, "wing" into "wing'd."

Carter's night sky likewise comes into view through the interplay of astronomical denotation and imaginative connotation. While the poet names Cassiopeia, Northern Crown, and Triones, which she annotates in an earlier version as "Constellations so call'd," the final constellation inaugurates a pictorial image of the stars' light assisting a ship's navigation (Carter, 1738: 315 n.). The stars' "faithful Beams" illuminate a path through uncharted waters for a "wand'ring Ship," a vessel that wanders just like the fancy that conjures it into poetic being, repeating, in the process, the homonymic connection to "wondering." Carter's poet playfully upends the association of the northern sea's icy waters with the image of a "wide Desart of the pathless Deep" (Carter,

1999: l. 10). The term "pathless" not only suggests that the sea has not been explored or traveled or charted but also that there is no way to do any of those three activities: the "wide Desart of the pathless Deep" is a space that resists instruments of scale and measurement, and is impervious to the disciplining of exploration and cartography. The "wide Desart of the pathless Deep" denotes seemingly unexplored artic waters; it simultaneously connotes a spatial plane beyond apprehension and calculation.

The sense of infinitude associated with the sea cascades through the poem. The "Wonders of the skies" are the stars. They are also the possibility of other worlds, that chestnut of philosophical contemplation, the plurality of worlds. As the specificity of named constellations gives way to a wider and more expanded sense of the sky, the horizon unfolds with never-ending worlds: "Throughout the *Galaxy's* extended Line, / Unnumber'd Orbs in gay Confusion shine" (Carter, 1999: ll. 12–13). The phrase "Unnumber'd Orbs" names but cannot number. If astronomy as a field of study requires cataloguing objects using the principles of mathematics and physics, aided by the workhorse labor of diurnal observation, then Carter's adjective "unnumber'd" shows limits of these practices and the need for alternatives. The "Wonders of the skies" offer a "Presence, unconfin'd by Time or Place" that "Fills all the vast Immensity of Space" (Carter, 1999: ll. 33–34). To apprehend what Carter describes requires the simultaneity of observation and imagination, opening up the eye and the mind to space far beyond human scale. And this experience is virtual, rendered through Carter's literary figurations. Carter's poetry sends readers into a spatial realm impervious to ordinary perception, requiring those same readers to know with wonder.

If Carter's poetry requires a recalibration of what spatial dimensions might be and how one experiences them, then Charlotte Lennox's midcentury periodical, *The Lady's Museum* (1760–61), brings this consideration not only to space but also to time. When Lennox encourages readers to study the natural world, she foregrounds an entanglement of movement and desire that harnesses wonder to explore, understand, and know it. In language evocative of Boyle's approach, natural philosophy is "the pursuance of an apparent horizon, the boundaries of which are ever flying before us, and although they every moment present us with a fresh variety of enchanting objects, yet are, with respect to ourselves, as absolutely distant at the last as the first moment of our journey" (Lennox, 1760–61: 2.857). This unending horizon presents a "fresh variety of enchanting objects" that span both the gigantic and the minute and that range over time and across geographies (Lennox, 1760–61: 1.133). The periodical's itinerary of natural philosophical study "transports our readers by turns through all the regions of earth, air, and ocean, and to different climates, with expedition beyond the power of a magician's wand" (Lennox, 1760–61: 1.132–33). Natural philosophical praxis must adjust: "No bars of time, of place, or distance, or *even impossibility itself*, shall stop our progress" (Lennox, 1760–61: 1.133, emphasis added). Experienced as an arc of pursuit, and reminiscent of Thomson's swain running to catch the elusive rainbow, natural philosophical study moves one through spaces and times in ways that challenge ordinary geographic and temporal boundaries. Just as the "variety" of the world recalibrates the coordinates of geography and time, so, too, does Lennox's phrase, "with expedition *beyond the power of a magician's wand*." To know with wonder is not magic, which stops short of the ambition and vision that Lennox presents. Knowing with wonder, instead, is the integrated praxis of observation and imagination that sees and understands beyond what we have come to know.

As "the wonders of Nature's inexhaustible storehouse" exceed human scale in all metrics, they require knowing with wonder (Lennox, 1760–61: 2.857). Only then might one perceive space and time anew. Take the familiar example of a caterpillar transforming into butterfly; Lennox describes the metamorphosis of a swallowtail butterfly, supplemented by a detailed engraving (Lennox, 1760–61: 2.467–74). That a single body can appear to be worm-like only to change over time completely into a flutter of jewel-like colors encapsulates wonder as a visibly transformative process. While the example of a butterfly is familiar, even if still transfixing, it also reminds readers that natural philosophical observation has a duration. Just as Gilbert White in *The Natural History of Selborne* describes making notes over twenty years to come to understand natural wonders, so, too, does any individual need to attend to the scale of time. The idea that natural philosophical observational praxis requires time is not surprising, of course. One need only recall the nocturnal observations and records demanded by astronomical study. Caroline Herschel's papers, for example, are filled with nightly astronomical records she collected for her own study and that of her brother, Sir William Herschel (Herschel mss., n.d.).

However, Lennox reconceives duration, entertaining the possibility that it, too, must be understood more amply, asking, how might one study a natural phenomenon *before* it becomes available to sensory perception, whether aided by scientific instrumentation or not? To develop an answer, Lennox selects the example of the "Ephemeron, or Day-Fly." The observable lifespan of this insect is five hours at most, leading to its name, "Day-Fly." The life of this insect might, in one sense, be understood as "the whole duration of which . . . is never more than about five hours, in which short space it generates, lays eggs, grows old, and dies" (Lennox, 1760–61: 2.640). Yet Lennox's eidolon insists that one cannot know the Day-Fly merely in its "fly-state": one must also understand and perceive the insect's material existence over time. Lennox argues that to do this requires connecting the hours of the fly's life to its "existence under another form, and in another element, which continues through a space of three years" (Lennox, 1760–61: 2.636). Lennox trains her focus on the unobservable pre-history of the day-fly, deep in the riverbed's slime. The fundamental connection between "an enlivened flutterer of the airy regions" and "his original existence ... in the waters" forces a reckoning: the five hours of the day fly cannot be separated from the three years of that earlier existence, the nature of which Lennox fully adumbrates over several pages (Lennox, 1760–61: 2.636).

In this seemingly inconsequential creature with its seemingly brief, furtive life, Lennox offers a narrative that houses ostensibly incommensurate temporal planes, both available through the knowing of wonder. To perceive the true lifespan of the day fly, one must observe and imagine its material existence in the mud and the air, over three years and five days, in the riverbed and the air. Lennox imagines space-time in flux and ever expanding, a potential that simultaneously unleashes new ways of seeing and comprehending the natural world, to know with wonder.

To know with wonder introduces a radical potential, whether realized or not.

7 Wonder's Subjunctive Mood

To know with wonder recognizes wonder as a sustained, cognitive activity that interweaves the close observation and imaginative thinking inherent to natural philosophical practice. To know with wonder is therefore simultaneously expansive and critical: it reveals a mode of apprehension and cognition in which one may begin to imagine a world where space and time are reimagined. And as we shall see, to know with wonder also introduces us to wonder's subjunctive mood.

Wonder's subjunctive mood is where and how relations can be lateral rather than hierarchical, where difference might be sustained rather than overcome.

Wonder's subjunctive mood is also where and how we can begin to apprehend wonder's potential for reconfiguring intellectual, social, and ethical orders.

Luce Irigaray writes, with her character wit, "We need to reread Descartes a little" (Irigaray, 1993: 72.) Implicitly echoing Smith's turn to Cartesian physics to think about Cartesian wonder, Irigaray argues, "We should think about the fact that all the philosophers ... have always been physicists" (Irigaray, 1993: 72). The study of matter is the study of atoms, those bits that make up the material world and that establish the physical relations between things. And for Irigaray, atomistic thinking, circuits, and atoms of energy are the figures that not only animate her recuperation of Cartesian wonder but also reveal and shape ethics (Irigaray, 1993: 72). The intersection of physics and philosophy is the point at which one apprehends wonder and its ethical implications, a formulation that reminds us of Smith's evocation of Cartesian physics and wonder two centuries earlier.

When she takes up the issue of wonder's first-ness – why and how can wonder be the first passion – Irigaray imagines the conditions that lead to wonder and, as a consequence, that inform its potential as model of ethical relations. Unsettling the origin of Cartesian certainty, Irigaray's wonder is a response not to something new and unknown but to loss, which takes the form of "a mourning for the self as an autarchic entity" (Irigaray, 1993: 75). For Irigaray, wonder requires the enabling fiction that the self that is autarchic, that is, absolute and despotic. Wonder, she teaches us, provides a story for the self's own history and also a *response* to that story of its own history (the response of mourning). But if wonder, as the original passion, initiates and responds to a feeling of loss, then it likewise situates that loss as an occasion of relating to others. When one loses oneself, one finds others. "Wonder must be the advent or the event of the other" and the acknowledgment of "an interval between [oneself] and the other" (Irigaray, 1993: 75, 73). Wonder is the self's awareness of both not being alone and being in relation to other things: this is "a separation without a wound, awaiting or remembering, without despair or closing in on the self" and "the moment of illumination – already and still contemplative – between the subject and the world" (Irigaray, 1993: 75, 77). She writes that wonder is "indispensable not only to life but also or still to the creation of an ethics" (Irigaray, 1993: 74).

Irigaray's wonder is a space-time where the self recognizes a separate self *in* the other, a perception that shatters the fiction of "autarchy." And she tracks the ethical possibilities of wonder through visual observation, the workhorse of empirical epistemology (Irigaray, 1993: 74). The self acquires awareness not solely through the mourning of a past wholeness and separation (that never were) but also through the realization of being an object to something else altogether. To wonder is to be able to imagine oneself as a self and, to the extent this is possible, in relation to an *other*: "Wonder is not an enveloping. It corresponds to time, to space-time before and after that which can delimit, go round, encircle. It constitutes an opening prior to and following that which surrounds, enlaces" (Irigaray, 1993: 81). As Marguerite La Caze explains, Irigaray's revision of Cartesian wonder is "based on accepting others' differences" (La Caze, 2013: 1).

Wonder's space-time makes visible the reordering necessary to imagine ethical sociability. For Sara Ahmed, as I note earlier in this volume, wonder calls us to take up "a different relation to the world in which we live," a process that she identifies as pedagogical and political (Ahmed, 2004: 178). The simultaneity of wonder's space-time institutionalizes a seeing of then and now, "radicalization of our relation to the past, which is transformed into that which lives and breathes in the present" (Ahmed, 2004: 180). In wonder's "'first-ness': the object that appears before the subject is encountered for the first time, or *as if* for the first time. It is hence a departure from ordinary experience; or, by implication, the ordinary is not experienced or felt at all" (Ahmed, 2004: 179).

Much adheres to that phrase, "as if," not least of which is the subjunctive mood. Wonder is a noun and verb that operate in the indicative as well as the subjunctive; wonder, in Ahmed's words, "is about learning to see the world as something that does not have to be, and as something that came to be, over time, and with work" (Ahmed, 2004: 180). The word *learning* instructs and evokes Cartesian wonder's pedagogy: wonder requires that one attend closely, that one acquire knowledge about the world not as it might seem, but as it is and – most radically – as it might be.

This is how we recognize that wonder requires one encounter the world with the imperative of the subjective: *as if.* The subjunctive is a verbal mood. It "refers to an action or state as conceived (rather than as a fact) and is therefore used chiefly to express a wish, command, exhortation, or a contingent, hypothetical, or prospective event" (*OED*, 1989: s.v.). The subjunctive is a possibility and it gestures to the future (Portner, 2018: 5, 70). Within seventeenth- and eighteenth-century grammar books, the subjunctive is also always relational (Phillips, 1706: 632; Coles, 1717: 306). In the words of William Turner in 1710, the subjunctive "depends upon another Verb in the same Sentence, either going before or coming after" (Turner, 1710: 13). The subjunctive, in other words, opens representational space to imagine what *might have been* and to imagine what *might be*.

The subjunctive animates the most vital recent critical engagements with the past. Saidiya Hartman's methodology of "critical fabulation" expands into and exploits the subjunctive, "(a grammatical mood that expresses doubts, wishes, and possibilities)," as does Lisa Lowe's concept of intimacy (Hartman, 2008: 11). Reading Stephanie E. Smallwood's *Saltwater Slavery*, Lowe names "the *past temporal conditionality* of the 'what could have been,' [which] symbolizes aptly the space of a different kind of thinking" (Lowe, 2015: 40). "Intimacy" helps us see how reading with wonder might reveal connections and reconfigurations, might create the space-time for new relations. Lowe provides us the powerful lesson that modern, Western liberalism embeds the global conditions upon which it depends. These relations are visible through "scenes of close connection in relation to global geography that one more often conceives in terms of vast spatial distances" (Lowe, 2015: 18). For Lowe, intimacy shows us that even the most commonplace of Western liberal formulations relies upon an unacknowledged, unarticulated global relationship, setting up an implicit contrast and hierarchy between modern liberal subjects, and those "that are forgotten, cast as failed or irrelevant because they do not produce 'value' legible within modern classifications" (Lowe, 2015: 17–8). The subjunctive mood of wonder unfurls these paths towards Chuh's illiberal humanisms. If science *qua* science reveals "failed attachments," as McKittrick teaches us, then the circuitry of science through wonder's subjunctive mood fires up relations, possibilities, pasts, futurities (McKittrick, 2021: 3, n. 5).

Wonder's subjunctive mood fires up radical potential.

Wonder's subjunctive mood brings us Frances Flood and self-amputating legs. Wonder's subjunctive mood also brings us Olaudah Equiano and a clock, an "iron muzzle," and a Davis quadrant. These are not narratives that necessarily adhere to the subjunctive mood in a grammatically disciplined sense. These are texts that activate the subjunctive mood's conceptual range, the subjunctive mood of wonder.

As if.

"Stop Reader, and a Wonder see" (Flood, 1723: 6).

So commands a 1723 pamphlet, *The Devonshire Woman; or, A Wonderful Narrative of Frances Flood*. The imperative to stop addresses two audiences at once – the reader of the published pamphlet and the reader of a gravestone in the Salford Churchyard etched with those same words.

"Stop Reader, and a Wonder see."

And the second imperative? What does the speaker of the pamphlet, the Devonshire Woman herself, self-identified as Frances Flood, want her readers to see?

"As strange as e'er was known, / My Feet drop'd off from my Body, / In the middle of the bone" (Flood, 1723: 6).

The story is a poor woman's experience of wonder at her own body. Presented on the half-title as "The Devonshire Wonder," the central character is both author and businesswoman; the pamphlet is specifically printed "for *Frances Flood*, and Sold by No Body but herself" (Flood, 1723: title page, 2). The wonder of Frances Flood's legs does not rely upon external authenticating authority – be it a witness, natural philosopher, medical practitioner, or some other judge – but instead on the first-person account of an individualized, feminized personage who publishes and profits from the tale *and sale* of her wonder. A few years after the publication of *The Devonshire Woman*, the story of Mary Toft giving birth to rabbits circulated widely and infamously, evident in texts such as *The Wonder of Wonders: or, A True and Perfect Narrative of a Woman near Guilford in Surrey, who was Delivered lately of Seventeen Rabbets*. For six weeks, the veracity of Toft's rabbit births was credited by various scientific and medical authorities. Toft's experience began in her village, encircled by the authorizing presence of village women (mothers and midwives). But once her fame grew, she was scrutinized by professional, educated men who were interested (and arguably, self-interested) in converting this wonder into a scientific fact, jockeying to increase their professional and social status in the process (Harvey, 2020: 35, 46, 49). In contrast to the avalanche of publications by others, Toft's own account exists only in three "confessions." In these, Toft's claims shift as she is subjected to increasing levels of interrogation (Harvey, 2020: 62–72).

The case of Mary Toft underscores a key difference of France Flood's tale of wonder. Rather than existing as an object for others to report, observe, and scrutinize, Flood is a subject who demarks the terms and significance of her experiences.

And her story? Flood contracts smallpox, loses both legs, and lives. "My Flesh was separated," she writes (Flood, 1723: 3).

Flood describes arriving to Saltford in Somerset from Devonshire on 23 January. She appears to be alone (she does not mention any companion) and describes having been ill with active small pox pustules for a little over five weeks. On 18 March, her left leg "broke off as though it were a rotten stick," with "little loss of blood, nor hardly any pain" (Flood, 1723: 4). Following a fruitless visit by a surgeon, "On the 24th [of March], about 6 in the morning, . . . I arose and opened the Cloaths I found my Leg was fallen from me" (Flood, 1723: 5). Painless and quick-healing, Flood's self-amputations present a body acting on its own accord. "I had no Surgeon for my help," Flood explains, "But God Almighty's Aid" (Flood, 1723: 6).

That Flood's legs just fall off and that she did not die – these form the crux of this wonder. The loss of Flood's legs reminds us of what Carmen Fracchia describes as "the Castilian miracle of the Black leg" in the pictorial arts of Hapsburg Spain. The allegory, rendered variously, features an Afro-Hispanic man suffering (or dead), having undergone an *in vivo* amputation of his leg, which is grafted onto an ailing white verger to cure him (Fracchia, 2019: 121–53). In the legend of the miracle, those who operate are saints, and the Afro-Hispanic man always loses his leg, brutally; the legend "allegorizes the violence of the institution of slavery and sets up the iconography of the enslaved Afro-Hispanic subject" (Fracchia, 2019: 121). The "miracle of the Black leg" is a violent religious allegory that haunts from Hapsburg Spain. While Flood's account does not explicitly evoke the violence of enslavement, the loss of her legs likewise demands a different form of knowing.

As the narrator and the subject of *The Devonshire Woman; or, a Wonderful Narrative of Frances Flood*, Flood utilizes wonder as a cognitive passion to see and understand the world and her place in it differently. Wonder, *The Devonshire Woman* teaches us, requires a form of reading that reorients the temporal and spatial worlds to train us to see anew, discloses social relations and the ethics that shape them, and challenges us to embrace wonder's subjunctive mood – not what is but what *could* be. Herein lies wonder's most radical potential.

The social and ethical contexts of *The Devonshire Woman* narrow to the inaction of the town's overseer, who, Flood specifies, twice refuses to assist her. Only after Flood's small pox pustules appear does the overseer act, closing off the barn where she had taken refuge and giving her ointment to treat her open wounds. Flood pauses her narrative to forgive the overseer's absence of charity and care, insisting that "I freely forgive all the parish" and that town officials "may be blameless of my misfortunes" (Flood, 1723: 3, 4).

Flood's inclusion of these events and her explicit absolution raise questions. If Flood had received the care she requested, then would her body have become a wonder? That is, with assistance from the parish, would Flood's body have *needed* to become a wonder? And in the absence of any support, is Flood's experience of wonder itself a form of ethical care, saving this clearly impoverished and ill woman when no one else would (or could)?

Although Flood's account introduces and does not answer these questions, their prominence within the narrative reminds us that wonder is always relational, whether as an object or a feeling.

What does this mean?

Something – that term Adam Smith uses – is a wonder only if it provokes the feeling of wonder in another entity. In this process, the label of wonder is retrospectively assigned to an object or phenomenon because of its effect on someone. Flood's account tightens this loop. Her self-amputating legs are, as objects, a wonder. Flood's narrative represents her own wonder as a cognitive emotion, and it demands that the reader experience the same. The social world imagined in *The Devonshire Woman; or, a Wonderful Narrative of Frances Flood* is simultaneously an ethical world. In Flood's narrative, we are challenged, as Julietta Singh describes "unthinking mastery," "to open ourselves to reimagining ways of relating to each other – to human, nonhuman, and inhuman to which (even when disavowed) we are mutually bound" (Singh, 2018: 7–8). And when Flood commands, "Stop Reader, and a Wonder see," she likewise challenges us to develop what Singh calls a practice of "vulnerable reading" (Singh, 2018: 22).

"Stop Reader, and a Wonder see."

Wonder's subjunctive mood presses the urgency of reimagining the past and our relation to it, with the hope of forging a more equitable future.

Not the world as it was or as it is, but the world as it could have been and as it could be.

As if.

Wonder's subjunctive mood shapes two key moments in Olaudah Equiano's 1789 *The Interesting Narrative of the Life of Olaudah Equiano, Or Gustavus Vassa, The African*. Both are from Equiano's childhood when he encounters scientific technology and when the possibilities of wonder's subjunctive mood reveal relations and subjectivities both as they are and as they could be.

Recalling his life as a young enslaved African boy in Virginia, Equiano summons the memory of being required to attend the sleeping plantation's enslaver by fanning him. In the enslaver's bedroom, Equiano observes a clock on the chimney, ticktocking noisily, hanging near a portrait. Surprised and apprehensive, Equiano interprets the clock and the portrait as instruments of surveillance that monitor his labor and behavior, concerned that they "would tell the gentleman any thing I might do amiss" (Equiano, 2018: 45). Equiano's rendering of the clock and the portrait resound with the white "slave patrols" he encounters in Savannah defined by their racializing surveillance – that is, white men surveilling and harassing Black men, women, and children, free and enslaved (Nicolazzo, 2021: 202–36). The ticking of the clock, in particular, convinces Equiano that "these people were all made up of wonders" (Equiano, 2018: 46). Alexander Dick suggests that wonder here produces anxiety in Equiano that "cannot be relieved until the observer is removed from it" (Dick, 2019: 243).

But when Equiano uses the phrase "all made up of wonders," he captures the intimacy of technology and terror that shape his life, registering his consciousness, and also his refusal, of being subjected to tyrannical and abusive power. Nor does Equiano's assessment emerge in isolation, but in recognition of the whole-scale system of saltwater slavery – its brutality, violence, fixedness

(Smallwood, 2007: 7–8). Not sentences before Equiano's depiction of the clock and wonder, he describes entering the house on his way to the enslaver's chamber. When he passes the threshold into the kitchen, he witnesses an enslaved woman with her head and face violently imprisoned with an "iron muzzle":

> I had seen a black woman slave as I came through the house, who was cooking the dinner, and the poor creature was cruelly loaded with various kinds of iron machines; she had one particularly on her head, which locked her mouth so fast that she could scarcely speak; and could not eat nor drink. I was much astonished and shocked at this contrivance, which I afterwards learned was called the iron muzzle. (Equiano, 2018: 45)

An instrument of pain, control, and humiliation, the iron muzzle imprisons this woman's head and face as she labors. Violently refused food for her own consumption – the iron muzzle was used to silence and to starve – this woman must prepare food for the enslavers to consume. And the iron muzzle itself, in Equiano's words, is "so well known as not to need a description," one of many instruments of torture "sometimes applied for the slightest faults" (Equiano, 2018: 63, 112).

Remember: just moments before, Equiano describes the enslavers as "made up of wonders." The textual proximity of this assessment and the never-ending cruelty of enslavers' enactment of saltwater slavery confirms the intimacy of the two. In Equiano's narrative, the existence of the enslaved woman tortured into silence and deprivation, her labor extracted are in intimate relation to the slavocrat's leisure and technologies of surveillance. They cannot be extricated from each other. Equiano's scene of wonder focuses on technology that monitors, surveils, threatens – the clock, the "iron muzzle." But when Equiano remembers thinking "these people were all made up of wonders," he calls forth the ethics of wonder's subjunctive mood, its potential for world-making.

In *The Interesting Narrative,* Equiano uses wonder's subjunctive mood to introduce the possibility of seeing the world *as it could be*, and does so in the space, time, and process of saltwater slavery, the Middle Passage. In so doing, Equiano refuses the Middle Passage's refusal.

The Interesting Narrative resounds with astonishment and terror, detailing and accumulating the inhumane conditions into which enslaved Africans were forced. It is, in Equiano's words, "a scene of horror almost inconceivable" (Equiano, 2018: 41). Imprisoned in the slave ship as cargo, enslaved Africans breathe a miasma of sickness, excrement, and death, chains galling their limbs, attacked with extreme violence by the hands and minds of white enslavers. Equiano was a little boy of eleven years old surrounded by death and dying. He was stolen, subjected to the ontological and physical violence of saltwater slavery's ever incomplete, always brutal efforts to transform him from boy, son, and brother into chattel. He remembers wishing for death himself: "I envied them the freedom they enjoyed, and as often wished I could change my condition for theirs" (Equiano, 2018: 41). The cruelties of saltwater slavery are not only multiple. They also multiply, with copious, seemingly innumerable effects for the enslaved Africans caught in its machinery – physical and emotional suffering, a perpetual state of alarm and subjugation, the destruction of kith and kin (Mallipeddi, 2016: 180–205).

Equiano's account graphically captures the casual brutality of the enslavers and the systemic violence of saltwater slavery. The enslaver sailors are just as likely to flog an enslaved African for refusing to eat as they are to throw leftover fish overboard rather than give it to the starving enslaved Africans watching them (Equiano, 2018: 38, 40, 41–42).

In the Middle Passage – on the ship, "a scene of horror almost inconceivable" – there would seem to be no time or space for an enslaved African to wonder.

In the Middle Passage, Equiano wonders, creating the space and time of Chuh's illiberal humanisms.

As if.

Wedged into this extraordinary account of the "horror almost inconceivable," Equiano turns to a navigational instrument that will later shape his lived experience as a sailor, the quadrant. Equiano writes:

> During our passage I first saw flying fishes, which surprised me very much: they used frequently to fly across the ship, and many of them fell on the deck. I also now first saw the use of the quadrant; I had often with astonishment seen the mariners make observations with it, and I could not think what it meant. They at last took notice of my surprise; and one of them, willing to increase it, as well as to gratify my curiosity, made me one day look through it. The clouds appeared to me to be land, which disappeared as they passed along. This heightened my wonder; and I was now more persuaded than ever that I was in another world, and that every thing about me was magic. At last we came in sight of the island of Barbadoes, at which the whites on board gave a great shout, and made many signs of joy to us. (Equiano, 2018: 42)

"The sea and the ship" in *The Interesting Narrative*, as Fred Moten teaches us, "are emblematic of encounter, the originary site of abjection, of the production or evocation of a shuddering affect" (Moten, 2018: 63). Moten's reading also challenges us to see that the ship-of-containment also contains the means of its own undoing: "the ship is that in which one must be contained and yet what the ship contains must always itself contain some dangerous supplement that enacts not so much the reversal of encounter, or the return of the gaze, but their prior refusal" (Moten, 2018: 71).

Equiano's scene of wonder – the sea and the ship – begins with an imagistic correspondence to the fish the enslaver sailors withhold from the enslaved Africans. These fish now fly, as do the clouds, turning Equiano's (and the reader's) attention from the despair and cruelty of the slave ship to the openness and heightened possibilities of the ocean sky, the openness and heightened possibilities that a reimagining of space and time unfolds, that a new set of social and ethical relations might portend.

Fredrick Douglass will later see these possibilities as he views ships in the Baltimore harbor.[12]

As if.

Equiano's wonder presages the inadequacy, the incoherence of saltwater slavery. When Equiano takes up the Davis quadrant, also called the "backstaff" (Bruyns and Dunn, 2009: 15–21), he sees what he takes for land in front of him disappearing from sight, a phenomenon that induces wonder: "this," Equiano writes, "heightened my wonder." The retrospective quality of *The Interesting Narrative* enables Equiano to explain seeing clouds for land while maintaining the sense of awe that he experienced, qualities that lead him to imagine himself in "another world" where "every thing about me was magic."

That other world comes to be punctured by the ship's arrival – temporally, in the narrative; grammatically, in the next sentence – to the slave colony of Barbados.

Barbados. It was the first English colony in the West Indies to begin sugar cultivation, for personal use as early as 1627 and as a commercial enterprise in the 1640s (Sheridan, 1974: 129). The largest population on the island consisted of enslaved African laborers: between 1640 and 1700, approximately 134,500 enslaved Africans were transported to Barbados and labored in horrific conditions to produce the sugarcane that fed British wealth and power (Sheridan, 1974: 132; Handler and Lange, 1978: 15).

Barbados. It was also a port in the history of British navigation. In 1763, twenty-five years before the publication of *The Interesting Narrative,* the British government assigned the astronomer and mathematician Nevil Maskelyne the task of sailing to Barbados to test three devices that had been designed to measure longitude, the final chapter in the decades' long response to the 1714 Longitude Act with its £10,000 reward (Sobel, 2007: 111–25).

Barbados. Slavocracy and plantocracy, naval technology and empire.

---

12 I am grateful to Mary Helen Washington for suggesting this important connection between Equiano and Douglass.

Equiano's four sentences occupy an uneasy place in the Middle Passage and *The Interesting Narrative*. They introduce the possibility for wonder when Equiano uses a piece of scientific equipment to view the world. Once could argue that this moment narrates a peculiar, even distracting detour away from the Middle Passage and the journey of saltwater slavery. But this moment challenges us to reimagine the coordinates of time and space, to see the past's colonial intimacies and their inextricability: the histories of longitude, colonization, and chattel slavery. Taken together, this is what April C. E. Langley names Equiano's "kaleidoscopic re-memory" (Langley, 2007: 97–138).

As he sails, as he writes, as he moves throughout the *Interesting Narrative*, Equiano imagines into being "the antislavery political world" as well as "the familial unity of all Africans to create fraternal alliances with blacks scattered in the Atlantic world" (Mallipeddi, 2016: 198, 224). As he sails, as he writes, as he moves throughout the *Interesting Narrative*, Equiano sees the futurity of wonder's subjunctive mood.

And yet.

Moten's Equiano challenges *us* – us readers today, that is – to read in wonder's subjunctive mood. Moten's Equiano is "Mad, smart-assed, atypical in affect, unsubjective in an abjection that is more and less than itself, still acting out in the refusal to act as if he knows his master, knowledge of freedom given in knowing all but nothing" (Moten, 2018: 71).

Moten's "Equiano establishes the transportation of enlightenment on a ship of tools" (Moten, 2018: 71).

Reading Moten's Equiano's "transportation of enlightenment on a ship of tools" teaches us to see – that is, to see with and to see through – Equiano's quadrant as a process that activates the radical potential of wonder. It presages, impressionistically, that wonder's subjunctive mood is an ethical critical practice, a possibility that the *Interesting Narrative* ultimately takes.

As if.

Wonder's subjunctive mood teaches us to imagine more by imagining futurity.

8 The Ends of Wonder

This is a book about wonder – as an object, as a feeling, as an invitation to study, and as a way of thinking. Wonder, as we have seen throughout, is at the heart of natural philosophical inquiry in the long eighteenth century, its inaugural provocation, its long-standing problematic. Wonder requires observation and imagination, operating together, if uneasily, to give shape to forms of knowledge, scientific, literary, and social. Wonder gives us the tools to think and read in a subjunctive mode, a way of thinking and relating that can create space for newly defined ethical relations across space, over time. This is, as McKittrick observes, "the difficult work of thinking and learning across many sites, and thus coming to know, generously, varying and sifting worlds and ideas" (McKittrick, 2021: 5).

To ground this work in the eighteenth century is to make the case that the field itself – as an object of inquiry, as a set of relational possibilities – urges us to reimagine what we do and how we do it. Stories about colonialism and chattel slavery have been told from the moment they were imagined as political, economic, and ideological possibilities. The familiar, official archives are filled with financial accounts and sentimental longings, assurances and hesitations. These official archives also demarcate who and what matters. And these strategies of self-justification find an uneasy partnership in the business-as-usual matter of eighteenth-century studies. Twenty years ago, Srinivas Aravamudan, who would go on to serve as president of the field's main professional organization, the American Society for Eighteenth-Century Studies, swatted away scholars' "nostalgia for a time before postcolonialism" because it "runs the risk of reinstituting an eighteenth-century studies lightened of its historical and cultural burdens" (Aravamudan, 2001: 618).

As I write this, I hear Christina Sharpe call to develop a "method of encountering a past that is not past," which she names "the wake and wake work" of "plotting, mapping, and collecting the archives of Black immanent and imminent death, and in tracking the ways we resist, rupture, and disrupt that immanence and imminence aesthetically and materially" (Sharpe, 2016: 13).

That is to say that the period's legacies, interventions, possibilities, and limits are still with us, casting a long shadow but also, perhaps, opening up new possibilities, wherein – as I quoted Chuh's words in the opening of this book – "mastery is displaced by the prompt to collective thought and subjects (critics) and objects (texts) are understood in their mutuality" (Chuh, 2019: 5). Sara Ahmed calls this "critical wonder," the fundamental recognition that "nothing in the world can be taken for granted" (Ahmed, 2004: 162).

I am not the first to proclaim that the long eighteenth century is not over. Joseph Roach teaches us that the Atlantic world is shaped by hauntings and repurposings, where the past is gone but not forgotten, with buried memories folded back into present-day performances. He calls this "surrogation" (Roach, 1996: 2–6). Eugenia Zuroski reminds us that "no one else knows just how long the 'eighteenth century' has been in quite the same way as Indigenous and Black communities in the settler colonial nation states established in that period. It's a century that refuses to stop" (Zuroski, 2020).

Evoking Serres' concept of "crumpled time," Chuh argues that "the presentness of the past is acutely apprehensible" in our present moment, which requires "reckoning with the conquest and colonialism, racism and cis-heteropatriarchy, upon which bourgeois liberalism is not only founded but also continues to operate" (Chuh, 2019: 20). And as Lowe concludes in *The Intimacies of Four Continents*,

> it is necessary to live within but to think beyond this received liberal humanist tradition, and all the while, to imagine a much more complicated set of *stories about the emergence of the now*, in which what is foreclosed as unknowable is forever saturating the "what-can-be-known." We are left with the project of imagining, mourning, and reckoning "other humanities" within the received genealogy of "the human." (Lowe, 2015: 175; emphasis added)

"Stories about the emergence of the now."

In 2023, the president of Guyana called for reparations, asking for financial compensation from the descendants of European enslavers (Mohdin, 2023), a call concurrent with a United Nations report recommending financial reparations for transatlantic slavery (United Nations, 2023). Also in 2023, a former MP, Antoinette Sandbach, asked to be removed from a scholar's research into the transatlantic slave trade, in effect willing herself to be gone *and* forgotten. Antoinette Sandbach is a descendant of a member of the plantocracy, Samuel Sandbach, a wealthy Liverpool merchant who owned plantations in the West Indies. Antoinette Sandbach stated that while "she is not sympathetic to her ancestor, and describes slavery as appalling," "she argues that she has a right to be forgotten" (Thomas and Nevett, 2023). As my colleague, Johnathan W. Gray, observed, Sandbach's desire to be forgotten cannot be separated from a desire to keep that "slavery descended" wealth for herself (Gray, 2023).

"Stories about the emergence of the now."

This century that refuses to stop conceptually and materially informs where I work as a teacher and as a researcher, as a mentor and as a colleague. The University of Maryland sits on the ancestral homelands of the Piscataway People, who were among the first in the Western Hemisphere. In the 1744 *Treaty held at the Town of Lancaster, in Pennsylvania*, representatives of the Six Nations and the colonial governments of Maryland and Virginia agreed to a border at the eastern foot of the Shenandoah Mountains (*Minutes*, 1851: vol. 4, 698–737). But the wording of the treaty, along with the 1609 charter of

Virginia, provided colonialists with legal cover to claim territory far beyond – cover, that is, to steal Native lands.

The University of Maryland campus today is dotted with buildings that recall an eighteenth-century history that is forgotten but not gone, their names referring to Indigenous and English colonial legacies: Susquehanna Hall, the home of the English Department for twenty years, comes from the Len'api for "Oyster River"; Pocomoke Hall, the Alquonquin for "black water," names the Pocomoke People; "Anne Arundel Hall," "Calvert Hall," and "St. Mary's Hall" allude to the first three counties founded by English colonists in the seventeenth century; and the dorm, Queen Anne's Hall, names the early eighteenth-century British monarch. The University sits within the boundaries of "Prince George's County," named for the queen's consort, Prince George of Denmark. Together, these names "name-to-forget." They evoke, only to obscure, the era in which large-scale settler colonialism and genocide devastated the tribal nations in modern-day Maryland.

"Stories about the emergence of the now."

The long eighteenth century also laid the groundwork for the formal construction of the University of Maryland in the mid-nineteenth century. The institution was built with wealth extracted from the seized lands of Indigenous communities and with wealth extracted from enslaved Black men, women, and children. Under the auspices of the 1862 the Morrill Act, the US government handed the ownership of 202,971 acres of Indigenous lands to the University of Maryland, land stolen through "violence-backed treaties and land seizures" (*Land Grab Universities*, 2020). These lands are located in modern-day Michigan, Kansas, and Minnesota (and elsewhere), and were sold in blocks for $112,504. These funds supported the conversion of Maryland Agricultural College, founded in 1856 by Charles Benedict Calvert, into the land-grant institution of today.

The first trustees of the University of Maryland were slavocrats. Eighty years later, Thurgood Marshall was refused admission to the law school.

The 1850 and 1860 censuses document twelve members of the Adams family, a Black family, in four households adjacent to campus. And Adam Francis Plummer was an enslaved Black man owned by the founder of the University, Charles Benedict Calvert, a step-nephew owned by his step-uncle. Adam Francis Plummer left us his diary (Berlin and the Students of History 429, 2009: 17, 28–29).

"Stories about the emergence of the now."

Newtonian natural philosophy, particularly evident in *Philosophiæ Naturalis Principia Mathematica* (*Mathematical Principles of Natural Philosophy*, 1687), included mathematical calculations that many understood as confirming the racist belief in a Eurocentric worldview (Pratt, 1992: 9–10,15–37; Bauer, 2003: 180).

Robert Boyle was the youngest son of an immensely wealthy earl from whom he inherited estates and properties that, especially following Cromwell's punitive measures towards Ireland in the 1650s, earned him annual rents of £3000 (Aubrey, 1898: 1.36–37). He later held a position as director of the East India Company, developing a publishing program to translate and export Bibles.

Just a few miles south of my institutional home, Dr. Alondra Nelson – a social scientist trained in American studies, a scholar of science, technology, and social inequity – served as the deputy assistant to President Joe Biden and acting director of the White House Office of Science and Technology Policy (OSTP) from 2021 to 2023. In her remarks upon her appointment, Nelson explained that COVID-19 "held up a mirror" to society: "Never before in living memory have the connections between our scientific world and our social world been quite so stark as they are today" and "As a Black woman researcher, I am keenly aware of who is missing from these rooms" (Nelson, 2021).

What, in the words of Josie Gill, "would it mean for us . . . to examine the institutional structures and orders of knowledge that we reproduce in our work, and to understand how this connects to the humans for whom we feel pity but might keep separate from our intellectual thought?" (Gill, 2018: 287).

"Stories about the emergence of the now."

To view my professional landscape as sedimented, as structured by violence and erasures, as supporting whiteness and white supremacy in various forms, requires a mode of criticism that not only conjoins observation with speculation but also reimagines ethical relations to the past as a way to imagine and manifest a more equitable future.

The past demands our full critical *and* creative attention. In her 1993 Nobel Prize lecture, Toni Morrison taught us that narrative is not "merely entertainment," but "one of the principal ways we absorb knowledge" (Morrison, 1995: 318). The past and its myriad archives, in this instance, the British long eighteenth century, demand new stories, new imaginings. The past and the present and the future, too – they demand our wonder.

References

Addison, Joseph and Richard Steele. (1965). *The Spectator*, 5 vols., ed. Donald F. Bond, Oxford: Clarendon Press.

Agazie, Gabriella, Akash Anumarlapudi, Anne M. Archibald et al. (2023). "The NANOGrav 15 yr Data Set: Evidence for a Gravitational-Wave Background." *The Astrophysical Journal Letters*, 951 (L8): 1–24.

Ahmed, Sara. (2004). *The Cultural Politics of Emotion*, Edinburgh: Edinburgh University Press.

Aït-Touati, Frédérique. (2011). *Fictions of the Cosmos: Science and Literature in the Seventeenth Century*, trans. Susan Emanuel, Chicago, IL: University of Chicago Press.

The Amazing Wonder; or a Full and True Relation. (1710). London.

Aravamudan, Srinivas. (2001). "Equiano Lite." *Eighteenth-Century Studies*, 34 (4): 615–19.

Arbuthnot, John. (1734). *ΓΝΩΘΙ ΣΕΑΥΤΟΝ, Know Your Self: A Poem*, London.

Aristotle. (1984). *The Complete Works of Aristotle: Revised Oxford Translation*, ed. Jonathan Barnes, Princeton, TX: Princeton University Press.

Aubrey, John. (1898). *Brief Lives*. 2 vols., ed. Andrew Clark, Oxford: Clarendon Press.

Bacon, Francis. (1857–74). *The Works of Francis Bacon*, 14 vols., ed. James Spedding, Robert Leslie Ellis, and Douglas Denon Heath, London: Longman, Green, Longman, & Roberts.

Baker, Henry. (1742). *The Microscope Made Easy*, London.

Baker, Richard. (1643). *Chronicle of the Kings of England*, London.

Bauer, Ralph. (2003). *The Cultural Geography of Colonial American Literatures: Empire, Travel, Modernity*, Cambridge: Cambridge University Press.

(2019). *The Alchemy of Conquest: Science, Religion, and the Secrets of the New World*, Charlottesville, VA: University of Virginia Press.

Behn, Aphra. (2021). *The Cambridge Edition of the Works of Aphra Behn. Volume IV, Plays 1682–1696*, ed. Rachel Adcock, Cambridge: Cambridge University Press, pp. 373–530.

Berlin, Ira and the Students of History 429. (2009). *Knowing Our History: African American Slavery & the University of Maryland*, College Park, MD: University of Maryland.

Blair, Patrick. (1717). "An Account of the Dissection of a Child." *Philosophical Transactions*, 30 (353): 631–32.

Boyle, Robert. (1660). *New Experiments Physico-mechanical, Touching the Spring of the Air, and Its Effects*, London.

(1661). *A Proemial Essay*, London.

(1662). *Defense of the Doctrine Touching the Spring and Weight of the Air*, London.

(1667). "Observables upon a Monstrous Head." *Philosophical Transactions*, 1: 85–86.

(1685). *Of the High Veneration Man's Intellect Owes to God*, London.

(1692). *The General History of Air*, London.

(1999–2000). *The Works of Robert Boyle*, ed. Michael C. Hunter and Edward B. Davis, 14 vols, London: Pickering and Chatto.

Breynius, Johannes Philippus. (1725). "Dissertatiuncula de Agne Vegetabile Scythico, Boramtez vulgo dicto." *Philosophical Transactions*, 33: 353–60.

Bruyns, W. F. J. Mrzer and Richard Dunn. (2009). *Sextants at Greenwich: A Catalogue of the Mariner's Quadrants, Mariner's Astrolabes Cross-staffs, Backstaffs, Octants, Sextants, Quintants, Reflecting Circles and Artificial Horizons in the National Maritime Museum, Greenwich*, Oxford: Oxford University Press.

The Buckinghamshire Miracle; or, the World's Wonder. (n.d.) London.

Buckle, Stephen. (2001). *Hume's Enlightenment Trace: The Unity and Purpose of an Enquiry Concerning Human Understanding*, Oxford: Clarendon Press.

Burns, William E. (2002). *An Age of Wonders: Prodigies, Politics and Providence in England 1657–1727*, Manchester: University of Manchester Press.

Butler, Samuel (1973). *Hudibras, Parts I and II and Selected Other Writings*, ed. John Wilders and Hugh de Quehen, Oxford: Clarendon Press.

Campbell, Mary Baine. (1999). *Wonder and Science: Imagining Worlds in Early Modern Europe*, Ithaca, NY: Cornell University Press.

Carter, Elizabeth. (1738). "While Clear the Night, and Ev'ry Thought Serene." *The Gentleman's Magazine*: 315–16.

(1999). "While Clear the Night, and Ev'ry Thought Serene." In *Bluestocking Feminism: Writings of the Bluestocking Circle, 1738–1785*, vol. 2, ed. Judith Hawley, London: Routledge, pp. 348–50.

Casid, Jill H. (2015). *Scenes of Projection: Recasting the Enlightenment Subject*, Minneapolis, MN: University of Minnesota Press.

Cavendish, Margaret. (2000). *The Description of a New World, Called the Blazing World*. In *Paper Bodies: A Margaret Cavendish Reader*, ed. Sylvia Bowerbank and Sara Mendelson, Peterborough: Broadview Press, 151–251.

Céard, Jean. (1977). *La nature et les prodigies: l'insolite au 16e siècle, en France*, Geneva: Droz.

Cheyne, George. (1740). *Essay on Regimen: Together with Five Discourses, Medical, Moral, and Philosophical*, London.

Chico, Tita. (2018). *The Experimental Imagination: Literary Knowledge and Science in the British Enlightenment*, Stanford, CA: Stanford University Press.

(2024). "Eighteenth-Century Science and Culture." In *Routledge Companion to Eighteenth-Century Literatures in English*, ed. Sarah Eron, Nicole Aljoe, and Suvir Kaul, London: Routledge, pp. 471–84.

Chuh, Kandice. (2003). *Imagine Otherwise: On Asian Americanist Critique*, Durham, NC: Duke University Press.

(2019). *The Difference Aesthetics: On the Humanities "After Man,"* Durham, NC: Duke University Press.

Clericuzio, Antonio. (2010). "'Sooty Empiricks' and Natural Philosophers: The Status of Chemistry in the Seventeenth Century." *Science in Context*, 23 (3): 329–350.

Coles, Elisha. (1717). *An English Dictionary*, London.

Collins, Samuel. (1671). *The Present State of Russia*, London.

Coppola, Al. (2016). *The Theater of Experiment: Staging Natural Philosophy in Eighteenth-Century Britain*, Oxford: Oxford University Press.

Cook, John. (1997). *Voyages and Travels through the Russian Empire, Tartary, and Part of the Kingdom of Persia*, ed., A. L. Fullerton, 3rd ed., Newtonville, MA: Oriental Research Partners.

Cuillé, Tili Boon. (2021). *Divining Nature: Aesthetics of Enchantment in Enlightenment France*, Stanford, CA: Stanford University Press.

Curry, Patrick. (1989). *Prophecy and Power: Astrology in Early Modern England*, Princeton, TX: Princeton University Press.

DeMaria, Jr., Robert. (2018). *British Literature, 1640–1789: Keywords*, West Sussex: Wiley Blackwell.

Dennis, John. (1704). *The Grounds of Criticism in Poetry*, London.

Descartes, René. (2015). *The Passions of the Soul and Other Late Philosophical Writings*, trans. Michael Moriarty, Oxford: Oxford University Press.

Dick, Alexander. (2019). Objects Taken for Wonders in Equiano's Interesting Narrative." In *Romanticism and Speculative Realism*, ed. Chris Washington and Anne McCarthy, London: Bloomsbury Academic, pp. 237–55.

A Dissertation on Royal Societies: In Three Letters. (1750). London.

Drummond, John. (1780). *The Art of Reading and Speaking in Public*, 2nd ed., Edinburgh.

Dyer, John. (1757). *The Fleece: A Poem*, London.

Ehrenberger, Bonifacius Heinrich. (1713). *Novum et curiosum laternae magicae augmentum*, Heidelberg.

Equiano, Olaudah. (2018). *The Interesting Narrative*, ed. Brycchan Carey, Oxford: Oxford University Press.

Evelyn, John. (1825). *Silva; or, a Discourse of Forest-Trees*, 2 vols., London: H. Colburn.

The Female American; or, the Adventures of Unca Eliza Winkfield. (2014). 2nd ed., ed. Michelle Burnham and James Freitas, Peterborough: Broadview Press.

Flood, Frances. (1723). *The Devonshire Woman; or, a Wonderful Narrative of Frances Flood*, Reading.

Floyer, John. (1707). *The Physician's Pulse Watch*, London.

Fournier, Marian. (1996). *The Fabric of Life: Microscopy in the Seventeenth Century*, Baltimore, MD: Johns Hopkins University Press.

Fracchia, Carmen. (2019). *"Black but Human": Slavery and Visual Art in Hapsburg Spain, 1480–1700*, Oxford: Oxford University Press.

Frank, Jr., R. G. (1980). *Harvey and the Oxford Physiologists: A Study of Scientific Ideas*, Berkeley, CA: University of California Press.

Gill, Josie. (2018). "Decolonizing Literature and Science," *Configurations*, 26 (3): 283–88.

Girten, Kristin M. (2024). *Sensitive Witnesses: Feminist Materialism in the British Enlightenment*, Stanford: Stanford University Press.

Gravesande, Willem Jacob 's. (1731). *Mathematical Elements of Natural Philosophy*, trans. John Theophilus Desaguliers, 2 vols., London.

Gray, Jonathan W. [@elmcitytree.bsky.social], August 31, 2023 at 5:41 PM, Bluesky. "In order to understand her discomfort you have to pair the article David quotes with this one. She's trying to keep that slavery descended $$."

Greenblatt, Stephen. (1991). *Marvelous Possessions: The Wonder of the New World*, Chicago, IL: University of Chicago Press.

Gregory, William. (1738). "An Account of a Pin Taken out of the Bladder of a Child." *Philosophical Transactions* 40 (450): 367–69.

Guerrini, Anita. (2000). Obesity and Depression in the Enlightenment: The Life and Times of George Cheyne, Norman, OK: University of Oklahoma Press.

Hacking, Ian. (1983). *Representing and Intervening: Introductory Topics in the Philosophy of Natural Science*, Cambridge: Cambridge University Press.

Hall, Marie Boas. (1956). *Robert Boyle and Seventeenth-Century Chemistry*, Cambridge: Cambridge University Press.

Hall, A. R. and M. B. Hall. (1969). "The Intellectual Origins of the Royal Society: London and Oxford." *Notes and Records of the Royal Society*, 23: 157–68.

Hall, David D. (1989). *Worlds of Wonder, Days of Judgment: Popular Religious Belief in Early New England*, New York: Knopf.

Handler, Jerome S. and Frederick W. Lange. (1978). *Plantation Slavery in Barbados: An Archaeological and Historical Investigation*, Cambridge, MA: Harvard University Press.

Haraway, Donna. (1997). *Modest_Witness@Second_Millennium.FemaleMan_Meets_OncoMouse: Feminism and Technoscience*, London: Routledge.

Harding, Sandra. (2008). *Sciences from Below: Feminisms, Postcolonialities, and Modernities*, Durham, NC: Duke University Press.

Hartman, Saidiya. (2008). "Venus in Two Acts," *Small Axe*, 12(2): 1–14.

Harvey, Karen. (2020). *The Imposteress Rabbit Breeder: Mary Toft and Eighteenth-Century England*, Oxford: Oxford University Press.

Herschel, Caroline. (n.d.) *Common Place Book*, M0672 n.d., Harry Ransom Center, Austin, TX.

Hill, Aaron. (1779). *Essay on the Act of Acting*, London.

Holmes, Richard. (2008). *The Age of Wonder: How the Romantic Generation Discovered the Beauty and Terror of Science*, London: Penguin Books.

Hooke, Robert. (1665). *Micrographia: Or Some Physiological Descriptions of Minute Bodies*. London.

(1668). "A Contrivance to Make the Picture of Any Thing Appear on a Wall, Cub-Board, or within a Picture-Frame, &c. in the Midst of a Light Room in the Day-Time; or in the Night-Time in Any Room That Is Enlightned [sic.] with a Considerable Number of Candles." *Philosophical Transactions*, 3: 741–743.

(1678). *Lectures de Potentia Restitutiva, or of a Spring Explaining the Power of Springing Bodies*, London.

Hume, David. (1992). *Enquiries Concerning Human Understanding and Concerning the Principles of Morals*, 3rd ed., ed. P. H. Nidditch, Oxford: Clarendon Press.

Hunter, Michael. (1982). *The Royal Society and Its Fellows, 1660–1700: The Morphology of an Early Scientific Institution*, Chalfont St. Giles: British Society for the History of Science.

(2003). "Robert Hooke: The Natural Philosopher." In *London's Leonardo: The Life and Work of Robert Hooke*, ed. Jim Bennett, Michael Cooper, Michael Hunter, and Lisa Jardine, Oxford: Oxford University Press, pp. 105–62.

Huygens, Christiaan. (1950). *Oeuvres complètes. Tome XXII. Supplément à la correspondance. Varia. Biographie. Catalogue de vente*, La Have: Martinus Nijhoff.

Irigaray, Luce. (1993). "Wonder: A Reading of Descartes, the Passions of the Soul." In *An Ethics of Sexual Difference*, trans. Carolyn Burke and Gillian C. Gill, Ithaca, NY: Cornell University Press, pp. 72–82.

Jarvis, J. Ereck. (2016). “The Royal Society, Collective Vision and Samuel Butler’s ‘*The Elephant in the Moon.*’” In *Literature in the Age of Celestial Discovery*, ed. J. A. Hayden, New York: Palgrave Macmillan, pp. 133–47.

Johnson, Samuel. (1755). *Dictionary of the English Language*, London.

Jones, Henry. (1746). *Philosophy. A Poem Address'd to the Ladies Who Attended Mr. Booth's Lectures*, Dublin.

Journal Book of the Royal Society. (1666). 2 vols., London.

Kareem, Sarah Tindal. (2014). *Eighteenth-Century Fiction and the Reinvention of Wonder*, Oxford: Oxford University Press.

Kircher, Athanasius. (1646). *Ars Magna Lucis et Umbrae*, Rome.

Kramnick, Jonathan. (2010). *Actions and Objects from Hobbes to Richardson*, Stanford, CA: Stanford University Press.

La Caze, Marguerite. (2013). *Wonder and Generosity: Their Role in Ethics and Politics*, New York: SUNY Press.

Land Grab Universities. (2020). *A High Country News Investigation.* www.landgrabu.org.

Langley, April C. E. (2007). *The Black Aesthetic Unbound: Theorizing the Dilemma of Eighteenth-Century African-American Literature*, Columbus, OH: Ohio State University Press.

Latour, Bruno. (1993). *We Have Never Been Modern*, trans. Catherine Porter, Cambridge, MA: Harvard University Press.

Lavoisier, Antoine. (1790). *Elements of Chemistry, in a New Systematic Order, Containing All the Modern Discoveries*, Edinburgh.

LeClerc, Daniel. (1721). *A Natural and Medicinal History of Worms Bred in the Bodies of Men and Other Animals*, trans. Joseph Browne, London.

Leeuwenhoek, Antoni van. (1708). “Microscopical Observations upon the Tongue.” *Philosophical Transactions*, 26: 114–23.

Leibniz, Gottfried Wilhelm. (1675). “Drôle de Pensée, touchant une nouvelle sorte de Representations,” mss., Eigenhändige Aufzeichnungen A, Leibniz Archiv, Niedersächsische Landesbibliothek, Hannover.

Lennox, Charlotte. (1760–61). *The Lady's Museum*, 2 vols., London.

Lewis, Jayne Elizabeth. (2012). *Air's Appearance: Literary Atmosphere in British Fiction, 1660–1794*, Chicago, IL: University of Chicago Press.

Lister, Martin. (1684). “A Letter Written to Mr. H.O. Concerning Some Very Aged Persons in the North of England.” *Philosophical Transactions*, 14: 592–98.

Lowe, Lisa. (2015). *The Intimacies of Four Continents*, Durham, NC: Duke University Press.

McKittrick, Katherine. (2021). *Dear Science and Other Stories*, Durham, NC: Duke University Press.

Mallipeddi, Ramesh. (2016). *Spectacular Sufferings: Witnessing Slavery in the Eighteenth-Century British Atlantic*, Charlottesville, VA: University of Virginia Press.

Martyn, J. (1729). “An Account of Some Observations Relating to Natural History, Made in a Journey to the Peak in Derbyshire.” *Philosophical Transactions*, 36 (407): 22–32.

Minutes of the Provincial Council of Pennsylvania. (1851). Harrisburg: Theo, Fenn.

Mohdin, Aamna. (2023). “Guyana’s president asks European slave traders’ descendants to pay reparations,” *The Guardian* (Friday, August 25, 2023). www.theguardian.com/world/2023/aug/25/guyanas-president-asks-european-slave-traders-descendants-to-pay-reparations.

Morrison, Toni. (1995). “*Nobel Lecture*, 7 December 1993.” *The Georgia Review*, 49 (1): 318–23.

Moten, Fred. (2018). *Stolen Life*. New York: New York University Press.

Nelson, Alondra. (2021). “Remarks as Prepared for Delivery by OSTP Deputy Director for Science and Society Dr. Alondra Nelson in Wilmington, Delaware,” *The American Presidency Project*. https://www.presidency.ucsb.edu/documents/remarks-prepared-for-delivery-white-house-science-team-nominees-and-appointees-wilmington.

Newton, Issac. (1687). *Philosophiæ Naturalis Principia Mathematica*, London.

Nicolazzo, Sal. (2021). *Vagrant Figures: Law, Literature, and the Origins of the Police*. New Haven, CT: Yale University Press.

O’Brien, Karen. (1999). “Imperial Georgic, 1660–1789.” In *The Country and the City Revisited: England and the Politics of Culture, 1550–1850*, ed. Gerald Maclean, Donna Landry, and Joseph P. Ward, Cambridge: Cambridge University Press, pp. 160–79.

Ogden, Emily. (2022). *On Not Knowing: How to Love and Other Essays*, Chicago, IL: University of Chicago Press.

Onions, C. T., ed. (1966). *The Oxford Dictionary of English Etymology*, Oxford: Oxford University Press.

Oxford English Dictionary. (1989). Oxford: Oxford University Press.

P.Q. (1742). *The Hampshire Wonder; or, the Groaning Tree*, London.

Park, Katharine and Lorraine Daston. (1998). *Wonders and the Order of Nature 1150–1750*, New York: Zone Books.

Park, Julie. (2023). *My Dark Room: Spaces of the Inner Self in Eighteenth-Century England*, Chicago, IL: University of Chicago Press.

Pennock, Robert T. (2019). *An Instinct for Truth: Curiosity and the Moral Character of Science*, Cambridge, MA: MIT Press.

Phillips, Edward. (1706). *The New World of Words: Or, Universal English Dictionary*, 6th ed., London.

Plato. (1901). *Theaetes*, vol. 4 of *The Dialogues of Plato*, trans. Benjamin Jowett, New York: Scribner.

Poovey, Mary. (1998). *A History of the Modern Fact: Problems of Knowledge in the Sciences of Wealth and Society*, Chicago, IL: University of Chicago Press.

Portner, Paul. (2018). *Mood*, Oxford: Oxford University Press.

Pratt, Mary Louise. (1992). *Imperial Eyes: Travel Writing and Transculturation*, London: Routledge.

Pumfrey, Stephen. (1995). "Who Did the Work? Experimental Philosophers and Public Demonstrators in Augustan England," *The British Journal for the History of Science*, 28 (2): 131–56.

The Record of the Royal Society of London for the Promotion of Natural Knowledge. (1940). 4th ed., London: Morrison & Gibb.

Reese, Hope. (January 3, 2023). "Delving into the Science of Awe." *New York Times* Section D, p. 6.

Reill, Peter Hanns. (2005). *Vitalizing Nature in the Enlightenment*, Berkeley, CA: University of California Press.

Roach, Joseph. (1996). *Cities of the Dead: Circum-Atlantic Performance*, New York: Columbia University Press.

Ruestow, Edward G. (1996). *The Microscope in the Dutch Republic: The Shaping of Discovery*, Cambridge: Cambridge University Press.

Schierbeek, A. (1959). *Measuring the Invisible World: The Life and Works of Antoni van Leeuwenhoek*, London: Abelard-Schuman.

Schmidgen, Wolfram. (2013). *Exquisite Mixture: The Virtues of Impurity in Early Modern England*, Philadelphia, PA: University of Pennsylvania Press.

de Seytres, Joseph, Marquis de Caumont. (1738). "A Letter from the Marquis de Caumont to Sir Hans Sloane." *Philosophical Transactions*, 40(450): 369–70.

Shapin, Steven and Simon Schaffer. (1985). *Leviathan and the Air-Pump: Hobbes, Boyle, and the Experimental Life*, Princeton, NJ: Princeton University Press.

Shapiro, Barbara. (2001). "Natural Philosophy and Political Periodization: Interregnum, Restoration and Revolution." In *A Nation Transformed: England after the Restoration*, ed. Alan Houston and Steve Pincus, Cambridge: Cambridge University Press, pp. 299–328.

Sharpe, Christina. (2016). *In the Wake: On Blackness and Being*, Durham, NC: Duke University Press.

Sheridan, Richard B. (1974). *Sugar and Slavery: An Economic History of the British West Indies, 1623–1775*, Baltimore, MD: Johns Hopkins University Press.

Singh, Julietta. (2018). *Unthinking Mastery: Dehumanism and Decolonial Entanglements*, Durham, NC: Duke University Press.

Sloane, Hans. (1698). "A further Account of the Contents of the China Cabinet Mentioned Last Transaction, p. 390." *Philosophical Transactions* 10: 461–62.

Smallwood, Stephanie E. (2007). *Saltwater Slavery: A Middle Passage from Africa to American Diaspora*, Cambridge, MA: Harvard University Press.

Smith, Adam. (1980). *Essays on Philosophical Subjects*, ed. W. P. D. Wightman and J. C. Bryce, Oxford: Oxford University Press.

Smith, Courtney Weiss. (2016). *Empiricist Devotions Science, Religion, and Poetry in Early Eighteenth-Century England*, Charlottesville, VA: University of Virginia Press.

Smollett, Tobias. (1989). *The History and Adventures of an Atom*. Introduction and notes by Robert Adams Day, text edited by O M, Brack Jr., Athens: The University of Georgia Press.

Sobel, Dava. (2007). *Longitude*, London: Bloomsbury.

Sprat, Thomas. (1722). *The History of the Royal Society of London, for the Improving of Natural Knowledge*, 3rd ed., London.

Stewart, Dustin D. (2023). "Birds in the Loop: Parish Boundaries and Extendable Belonging." *Representations* 164 (1): 23–50.

Stewart, Larry. (1999). "Other Centres of Calculation, or, Where the Royal Society Didn't Count: Commerce, Coffee-Houses and Natural Philosophy in Early Modern London." *The British Journal for the History of Science*, 32 (2): 133–53.

de Superville, Daniel. (1740). "Some Reflections on Generation, and on Monsters, with a Description of some particular Monsters." *Philosophical Transactions* 41 (456): 294–307.

Thomas, Ed and Joshua Nevett. (2023). "Antoinette Sandbach: Ex-MP Asks to Be Removed from Slavery Research," *BBC News*, August 31, 2023. www .bbc.com/news/uk-66648763.

Thompson, Helen. (2017). *Fictional Matter: Empiricism, Corpuscles, and the Novel*, Philadelphia: University of Pennsylvania Press.

Thomson, James. (1981). *The Seasons*, ed. James Sambrook, Oxford: Clarendon Press.

A Treaty held at the Town of Lancaster, in Pennsylvania, By the Honourable the Commissioners for the Provinces of Virginia and Maryland, with the Indians of the Six Nations. (1744). Philadelphia.

Turner, William. (1710). *A Short Grammar of the English Tongue; for the Use of English Schools*, London.

Twells, Alison, Will Pooley, Matt Houlbrook, and Helen Rogers. (2023). "Undisciplined History: Creative Methods and Academic Practice." *History Workshop Journal*, 96: 153–175.

United Nations. (2023). "Implementation of the International Decade for People of African Descent: Report of the Secretary-General." A/78/317 General Assembly. https://documents.un.org/doc/undoc/gen/n23/245/15/pdf/n2324515.pdf.

Väliaho, Pasi. (2022). *Projecting Spirits: Speculation, Providence, and Early Modern Optical Media*, Stanford, CA: Stanford University Press.

Voltaire, M. de. (1738). "M. Voltaire to the Marchioness du CH**." In *The Elements of Sir Isaac Newton's Philosophy*, trans. John Hanna, London, pp. iii–viii.

Watts, Isaac. (1739). *The Doctrine of the Passions*, 3rd ed., London.

West, Emily M. (2023). "Technology, Temporality, and Queer Form in Horace Walpole's Gothic." In *British Literature and Technology, 1600–1830*, ed. Kristin M. Girten and Aaron R. Hanlon, Lewisburg, PA: Bucknell University Press, pp. 99–122.

Weston, Phoebe. (2023). "'Rude magnificence' Restored: Following in the Footsteps of Pioneering Naturalist Gilbert White," *The Guardian* (July 27, 2023). www.theguardian.com/environment/2023/jul/27/gilbert-white-pioneering-naturalist-rude-magnificence-restored-aoe.

Whalley, John. (1713). *A Full, True, Distinct and Perfect Account of the Prodigy, Which with Wonder and Amazement was Observed at Dublin*, Dublin.

White, Gilbert. (2013). *The Natural History of Selborne*, ed. Anne Secord, Oxford: Oxford University Press.

Wilson, Catherine. (1995). *The Invisible World: Early Modern Philosophy and the Invention of the Microscope*, Princeton, NJ: Princeton University Press.

The Wonder of Nature: Or Europe's Miracle. (1701). London.

The Wonder of Wonders: or, A True and Perfect Narrative of a Woman near Guilford in Surrey, who was Delivered lately of Seventeen Rabbets. (1726). Ipswich.

Yang, Chi-ming. (2021). "The Song of the Rice Bird, a Plantation Ekphrasis." *Eighteenth-Century Fiction*, 34 (1): 87–99.

Yang, Chi-ming and Sarah Rivett. (2021). "Invention: The Raven and the Bobolink: An American Fable," *Early American Literature,* 56 (2): 329–50.

Zahn, Johann. (1702). *Oculus artificialis teledioptricus sive Telescopium*, Nuremberg.

Zuroski, Eugenia. (2020). "*This Ship We're In*," *The Rambling* 9. https://the-rambling.com/2020/08/07/issue9-zuroski/.

(in press 2025). *A Funny Thing: The Undisciplined Eighteenth Century*, Cambridge: Cambridge University Press.

Acknowledgements

Wonder, as I discuss throughout these pages, is a noun and a verb, charged with particular urgency in its entanglements with natural philosophical theory and practice throughout the long eighteenth century. This topic, this approach, these questions have oriented my work – in the fullness of what that means – these last several years. They have guided me in ways that I am only now able to take in.

I thought I would complete this book while on leave in the spring of 2020. But then, as everyone reading this knows, the world turned upside down and it lurched. I was called back to work to help with the so-called pivot to online instruction. I took on new administrative leadership as director of a center, taught the incoming "Covid" graduate cohort, served on the ASECS executive board, and relaunched and served as president for the campus faculty organization to fight for improved labor conditions on campus. Mine is a diasporic family: national borders were newly monitored and surveilled; they were also chaotically closed. There were health problems, the weight and work of eldercare, the expansive labor of taking on more and more because, well, there were so many things to do. And so, four years later, I am finishing.

What does any of this have to do with wonder?

Wonder, as I discuss throughout these pages, is an affective and intellectual mode. It offers the possibility of recognizing relations and relationality, of forging new, unimagined connections, and of expanding into possibilities far beyond the scope of what has been. Through the circuitry of science as an area of inquiry and also as a process, my study of wonder reveals an eighteenth-century legacy that persists. In this lingering, the wonder I study has the potential to provide conceptual tools for a critical, intellectual practice that accounts for the past in ways that point to a better future. These last years have deepened my understanding of and commitment to these futurities.

Wonder is also about relations, and I am rich with them. I am grateful to all who have read, talked, and thought with me, including Dave Alff, Nicole Aljoe, Kat Alves, Em Anderson, Amanda Bailey, Rebecca Barr, Jennie Batchelor, Ralph Bauer, Dorothee Birk, Alison Conway, Bob DeMaria, Gillian Dow, Lisa Freeman, Michael Hanchard, Chad Infante, Tom Jones, Elaine McGirr, Ruth Mack, Ramesh Mallipeddi, Lisa Moore, Nush Powell, Joe Roach, Laura Stevens, Rajani Sudan, David Taylor, Helen Thompson, Courtney Weiss Smith, Chloe Wigston Smith, Danielle Spratt, Rajani Sudan, Chi-ming Yang, and Gena Zuroski – and especially Laura Brown, Luisa Calé, Lucinda Cole, Markman Ellis, Matt Kirschenbaum, Nicole King, Bob Markley, and Kellie

Robertson. My many thanks, too, to Eve Tavor Bannet and Markman, for their editorial vision and generosity, to the press's reviewers, Bob Markley and the anonymous reader, and to Krithika Shivakumar and the production team.

I am grateful for opportunities to present my work, amazed and inspired by the questions and conversations audience members have brought with them to the Folger Institute, the Juxtapositions Annual Lecture at the University of Buffalo, Leibniz University (Hannover, Germany), the Dibner Lecture in the History and Culture of Science at the Huntington Library, the Bloomsbury Lecture at Birkbeck University, the University of Cambridge, the Paul Gottschalk Memorial Lecture at Cornell University, and Princeton University.

To my intimates whose minds and hearts inspire, Alyssa Alston, Kandice Chuh, Bill Cohen, Cristobal Silva, Mary Helen Washington, and Janelle Wong, thank you.

To the women who have become like sisters over these many years, with whom I think in countless ways, Megan Nelson, Zita Nunes, Robin Peck, and Filiz Turhan, thank you.

To Gisela and Alejandro, Susana, Florencia and Eric, Sebastian, Stevie, and Tomás, thank you.

To Luz Amparo Reina, who helps takes care of my mother, thank you.

To my mother, Mumsie, my brothers, Greg and Matt, my in-laws, Laura and Adam, and my nephews, Ben and Dylan, thank you.

To Alex, who lives wonder daily with me, I dedicate this volume with all my love.

Cambridge Elements

Eighteenth-Century Connections

About the Series

Exploring connections between verbal and visual texts and the people, networks, cultures and places that engendered and enjoyed them during the long Eighteenth Century, this innovative series also examines the period's uses of oral, written and visual media, and experiments with the digital platform to facilitate communication of original scholarship with both colleagues and students.

Cambridge Elements

Eighteenth-Century Connections

Elements in the Series

Science and Reading in the Eighteenth Century: The Hardwicke Circle and the Royal Society, 1740–1766
Markman Ellis

Eighteenth-Century Illustration and Literary Material Culture: Richardson, Thomson, Defoe
Sandro Jung

Making Boswell's Life of Johnson: An Author-Publisher and His Support Network
Richard B. Sher

Pastoral Care through Letters in the British Atlantic
Alison Searle

The Domino and the Eighteenth-Century London Masquerade: A Social Biography of a Costume
Meghan Kobza

Paratext Printed with New English Plays, 1660–1700
Robert D. Hume

The Art of the Actress
Fashioning Identities

A Performance History of The Fair Penitent
Elaine McGirr

Labour of the Stitch: The Making and Remaking of Fashionable Georgian Dress
Serena Dyer

Early English Periodicals and Early Modern Social Media
Margaret J. M. Ezell

Reading with the Burneys: Patronage, Paratext, and Performance
Sophie Coulombeau

On Wonder: Literature and Science in the Long Eighteenth Century
Tita Chico

A full series listing is available at: www.cambridge.org/EECC

For EU product safety concerns, contact us at Calle de José Abascal, 56–1°, 28003 Madrid, Spain or eugpsr@cambridge.org.

www.ingramcontent.com/pod-product-compliance
Ingram Content Group UK Ltd.
Pitfield, Milton Keynes, MK11 3LW, UK
UKHW022144080726
473066UK00010B/750

* 9 7 8 1 1 0 8 7 9 2 6 4 6 *